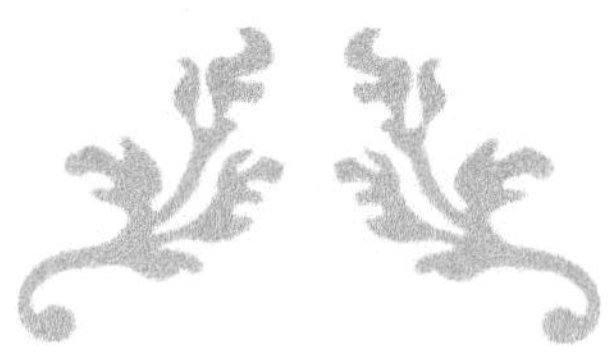

CHRISTMAS COUNTDOWN, SLIGHTLY CRACKED

[Document subtitle]

Eileen Buchheit

and Brenda Dean Shull, Ph.D.

Published in Dallas, Texas and Bridgewater, Connecticut by Maiden Voyage.

Subjects: Women—Religious aspects—Christianity/Christian women—Christmas—Revitalize

Printed in the United States of America

For our children and grandchildren who have given a lifetime of memories and laughter.

For our friends who have remembered our song when we forgot the words.

For our sweet husbands, David and Joe, who helped our resilience through life's challenges and kept a smile in our heart.

Ready or Not

We all remember the child's cry of "Ready or Not, here I come." How many of us, if we're honest, remember the panic we feel in the game of hide and seek. We usually aren't ready.

And so it goes with Christmas.

With its hustle, fast pace and family emphasis, we have learned to keep our friends close, our children closer and receipts for all major purchases in a secured place. As Dave Berry said," Once again we come to the Holiday Season, a deeply religious time that each of us observes, in his own way, by going to the mall of his choice." Or now, it is online hustle.

Of course, for women, it is multiple trips to the mall or computer time online. Santa gets all the credit.

For men, it is relaxing when there are only 14 shopping days left until Christmas, because that means they have 13 more days to relax.

I remember as a little girl watching my dad trying to wrap a perfume bottle the night before Christmas. We were hiding out in the bathroom to "surprise" my mother with her favorite (and requested) perfume. He fumbled with the paper. I was too little to help. His all- thumbs- wrapping toppled the bottle. It crashed into the sink.

The bottle shattered; the stench rose, filling the bathroom and wafting into the hall. My dad sheepishly looked down at me and smiled saying, "Well, that's the magic of Christmas. It's an exciting time of year when I find out what I'm getting your mom for Christmas. This broken glass will really surprise her. It's not exactly what she asked for."

And yet, Lo, He comes! Somewhere in the traffic jams (and you haven't even gotten out of the parking lot), and inevitable tonsillitis for your child in this allergy season (and throwing up by the dog because he chewed a decoration on the tree) with your cat up in the tree, the real reason for the season emerges!

As we see in the Gospel John, Jesus had been performing miracles or signs that made people question whether he was God's Son. As Jesus looked up and saw a crowd (or a mob of 5000 men plus women and children), He made the choice. The disciples wanted him to send the crowd away. But he saw Sheep without a Shepherd. There were people who needed to be fed, both physically and spiritually. He proceeded to supply food for 5000. In the push and shove of the masses, He gave resources for abundance. That is what he is still doing today. Lo, He comes.

Consequently, as two longtime friends, Eileen and Brenda have compiled memories in Christmas letter form for over the last 30 years. From the ghosts of Christmas past, comes a warm and witty account of two families' adventures. Here is our intention. We want to provide you a daily reading. We suggest reading one of our annual Christmas letters per day. If read daily, you can eventually time travel to Christmas current, getting a small boost of humor or hope to help you in your day. Perhaps you'll be able to relate and recall your own stories. Before you know it, Christmas is here. You will have had a chance to reflect with discussion questions and have a greater excitement of Christmas. We invite you to join us in the journey of not only who we are, but Whose we are. Through humor and a grateful heart, we are ready for Christmas!!

You may wonder at the title. We call this "Christmas Countdown, Slightly Cracked" because we are experts in the frenzy that takes a meaningful holiday and blows it up. All is calm? Not at our houses. Like most families, our celebrations are imperfect—good intentions but slightly cracked!

Eileen is from the North; Brenda is from the Southwest. Eileen was a brunette; Brenda is a blonde (roots don't count). Eileen is Catholic; Brenda is Protestant. We both speak English, but it doesn't sound that way. We met in Virginia over 45 years ago as young newly married wives sending our husbands off to the Army. It was unsettling because Viet Nam was still in the picture. Through the years our friendship has grown in wisdom and stature (We will ignore the stature; it's not fat. It is called fluffy.) We have been friends through thick and thin; well, we're not so sure about the thin. We no longer are what we were. We're sure we're improved versions.

We enjoy our look at life. As Amy Grant sang, "We are no longer what we were, but not all that we will be." We think we have grown in wisdom, and we're excited to step out of our comfort zone for what we can be. Want to join us?

Let's begin long ago and far away in 1986. The characters are the Shull family in Fort Worth, Texas. The Buchheit family is in Monterey, California as they prepare for a move to Rome, Italy.

Come with us as we open a time capsule.

As we look back, it is bittersweet. Today Eileen and Brenda know what happened. But Life provides a mystery. Not all the characters will make it to the present day. There will be birth and death. But, dear reader, no fair peeking ahead! Remember, this is a Christmas countdown. Adventure with us. By the end we believe that you, too, will be ready to rethink, reimagine, reinvent, revitalize Christmas.

Christmas Countdown, 1986

From Brenda: It all started when I sat down to write my Christmas cards. A prolonged "Mommy" proceeded Vance's entry into the room. Wisps of white-blond hair protruded from under his ski cap as he struggled with the zipper on his coat. This is Fort Worth, Texas in November where the temperature might possibly dip from the seventies to the sixties. At eight years old, Vance is the youngest of my three sons. Wearing a ski cap and coat in November-Texas weather is a little mystifying. This is my first clue.

"It's too small," he announced with his sky-blue eyes (like his dad's) flashing his frustration. Vance is my "planner" and he is already trying on his ski outfit. We plan to go to a Colorado cabin at Christmas so the boys can experience a White Christmas. Last year we took them for their first ski trip to Ruidosa, New Mexico. They skied better on the third day than it had taken us three years to acquire as adults. However, it was, after all, man-made snow. This time we were driving further north to Colorado.

Unfortunately, last year in New Mexico it was not snow cold. My bad!

I had over-bundled the boys to protect them from what turned out to be luke-warm cold weather. It only took a few minutes before Justin (second son) keeled over in the snow with heat and altitude sickness. Fortunately, we immediately corrected and lightened the outfits to fit the climate. Basically, on that first ski trip we got tans instead of snowflakes. This year we are optimistic that we will have frosty noses and snowball fights for Christmas in Colorado.

Vance, my second grader, is also my consumer. He exited the room with, "I really need a new one." I, on the other hand, have hopeful visions of a hand me down from his brothers.

Turning back to my Christmas cards, lovingly stacked on my desk, and awaiting my attention, I could hear the thudety clump of Justin outside. He is a slim, athletic fourth grader who plays whatever sport that is in season. It is now soccer, so he is practicing his kicks against the garage door. Soon it will be basketball, then baseball. He doesn't admit that he likes girls, but I have seen him spending time combing his straw blonde locks just perfectly, rolling up his sleeves and jean cuffs in an officially cool style. His younger brother Vance, of course, is watching and taking tips. Then Mr. Cool doesn't want to be too perfect and goes off to school with a long shirt tail dangling over his pants. It's the style.

But wait. The thump of the ball isn't the only sound. Wafting from the upstairs is the sound of a lovesick moose. It is Derek practicing his newly rented school saxophone. There are moments of musical notes. Surely it will get better. Mostly I fear a thundering herd of moose clattering up the lawn to return his call. (That would be a long trek to Dallas). He's pacing back and forth upstairs getting his practice in. He is now in the 6th grade which is middle school, and he is attempting the band. He says he is looking forward to the 7th

grade in hopes of the basketball team. Finding where you fit in middle school is tough. Tall for his eleven years, he prefers the Scouts where he enjoys once a month week-end camp outs. School and long homework assignments mercifully fade from his outdoors-away-from-it-all tent. Mad-libs and the outdoors reign in his scouting troop experience. This away-from-it all is much more to his liking.

David, my husband, pops his head in the room to remind me that he is going to be outside hanging the Christmas lights. The annual family joke is that we must beat our neighbors across the street in getting our lights hung first. If they see us, they, too, will fly into action. The Christmas miracle is not only finding the old nails along the roof to drape them, but a double miracle to see if the lights still work. This is going to stop the noise, because when the boys see David with a ladder and the ability to climb on the roof, they will be eager to help. As a mother, I don't want to see that wobbling roof action. On the other hand, when David pulls out the lawnmower, their fascination and willingness to help is not so intense. They are not quite so visible to their dad.

I mention to David that I can see that he has a fresh haircut. He grins and says his thinning hair just makes his shoulders look bigger. In his early forties, he is starting to get a tinge of gray, but he quips that he is just thankful for hair! He reminds me that the wish list for the boys this year is Skateboard, Nintendo games and an improbable photon laser toy of the 1986 variety. Maybe the skateboard will work for Derek and Nintendo games for Justin and Vance. Christmas is magical. Have you noticed that it creates a disappearing act? The disappearance is your money wisely spent.

It has been a good year for me. I have been teaching three classes as an adjunct professor at Texas Christian University in Fort Worth. I was asked to be a guest speaker on Time Management at the Tennessee Valley Women's Retreat in Guntersville, Alabama. I also did some time management seminars with my friend Sandy in Washington D.C. and New York City.

So now you have met my family at Christmas, 1986.

Meanwhile, let's meet Eileen's family at Christmas in 1986 in Chesterfield, Missouri. They are finishing a three-year assignment in suburbia rather than a military post or international assignment that they have had in the past. It provided a stable existence of church and scouts with school located only a few blocks away.

Writing Christmas letters is a long time Military tradition because it is the only way to keep up with friends from past military assignments. As we join Eileen in 1986, you meet Eileen, her husband Joe and two children, Brigid and Brett.

Eileen says:

Life in Chesterfield takes on a somewhat Norman Rockwell image. The cost of living is stable. The business community is welcoming to new ideas and houses grow on the hillside overnight. If you can leave out floods, tornadoes, and earthquakes (all of which we have experienced), it is an ideal existence. We've been here three years in June. This has been a lovely assignment, but we know it will be ending soon. We've begun thinking about our next move. When we left Germany, our orders said we were going to "to be announced." Perhaps we'll go to "to be announced" again.

Joe has been busy with his job in Project Management as ABSCOM "Aviation Systems Command." Friends are confused by St. Louis as a military assignment because there is no fort or base. Just large office buildings. For years my cousin George has questioned his mother about the weird assignments that Joe has received. He finally said, "Come on, Mom, tell me the truth. He's CIA, right?" The truth of the matter is, when Department of the Army calls, Joe says he'll have to get back to them. Immediate field positions get filled. This leaves Joe ready for more interesting ones like ABSCOM. No officers club. No command performances. Just hard work.

As for me, I have been teaching at St. Louis University's ESL program. Many of those students come from Arab countries. I've been learning a great deal about cultural differences when dealing with these students. They come to my house twice a year. Once in the Fall to celebrate an American family traditional Thanksgiving. Then in the Spring they come for what we loosely call Easter. To see grown men in long Arab robes hunting for Easter eggs and bribing Japanese students so they can have the most eggs in the basket is an eye-opening experience.

I made two New Year's Resolutions last year. One is reflected by this letter. One woman's small step into computer literacy. We bought an Apple and I seem to be the only slow learner in the family. I'm still plugging away while the rest of the Buchheits zoom along.

The other resolution had to do with aerobic classes. I've been going three times a week, hiding in the back row since January. Joe joins me on a regular basis, and we make the orthodox fitness fanatics crazy with our own versions of their serious exercise routines. Ours is improv. It includes do-si-dos and blowing kisses when we lose track.

The kids are fine and doing well. Brigid is 14. She attended a special Girl Scout Equestrian program last summer. The love of horses lives on. Brett at 12 is still very involved in Scouts. He and Joe shared summer camp fun together.

As you can see from this first glimpse, we are both happy families in our Christmas preparations and movement into the new year. It seems appropriate at this stage of the journey to turn to Jeremiah 29: 11-14. "For *I know the plans I have for you, "declares the Lord, "plans to prosper you and not to harm you, plans to give you hope and a future. Then you call upon me and come and pray to me and I will listen to you. You will seek me and find me when you seek me with all your heart. I will be found by you, "declares the Lord, "and will bring you back . . .from all the nations* **...".**

Let's Talk!

This is the start of our journey together in our Christmas countdown.

1) *If you are experiencing changes in your Christmas traditions, are you meeting it with great anticipation? What changes are happening in your Christmas?*

2) *Are you looking forward to this Christmas season? Are you serene on the outside but straining on the inside? Or is it your favorite time of the year?*

3) *Have you asked the Lord what plans He has, to prosper you and not to harm you, to give you hope and a future? What might those plans look like? Moving to a new location?*

4) *What part does attitude play in your Christmas plans?*

Christmas Countdown, 1987

"Give us the eyes of faith that we may see what God is about and that we may be about His work."

From Brenda: It's a Sunday afternoon and we're about to decorate our Christmas tree. It's a good time to let you peep in the window at our family to see how we are doing in 1987.

Derek, at 12, doesn't have as much trouble reaching the taller branches. He is almost as tall as me. How can he be almost taller than me? Brushing his curling sandy brown hair from his eyes (which gives him fits in the morning since he has discovered girls), he reaches for an ornament that Aunt Debbie made for him when he was a baby. For the moment his school worries are behind him. That's one of the joys of Christmas vacation. No school. Being a typical 7th grader, he hasn't quite gotten the hang of middle school. At this point, there are signs of the middle school misery. The question is—has middle school gotten *him*?

Justin is rustling in the Christmas box to select an ornament with his name on it. His white- blonde hair is changing to darker shades. He is wearing a popular coca cola shirt and has the collar turned just right. He's collecting baseball cards and dreams of the day when his own picture is on a card. As a fifth grader, he has decided to become a professional baseball player. He started reading the newspaper daily at the age of eight. But his reading the paper was totally focused--the Sports page only.

An infectious chuckle brings my attention to Vance. Almost as tall as Justin, he is nine and his flashing blue eyes are not fastened to athletics like Justin, but to Nintendo video games. He is finding it hard to tear himself away from "one last game" where he has "almost got it" to helping us hang ornaments on the tree. For such a smart child, he cannot read my lips, "No, you cannot have a go cart." He is always thinking of projects for David to help him build.

In comes Blue Eyes himself. David brings the Christmas lights, disentangled for the moment. We were delighted this summer when his work took him to California. We got to visit Disneyland!

As a matter of fact, I must tell you how we happened to get to Disneyland, because I believe it was a God wink. It also tells you about the type of man I married. David and our oldest son Derek were on the way to Boy Scouts when they saw a briefcase sitting in the middle of the neighborhood road. Pulling over, David picked it up and tossed it in the backseat because they were in a hurry to get to the Scout meeting. After the meeting he opened the briefcase to look for the owner's card so he could take it to the owner's home. When David and Derek pulled up to the home, they saw that the police were already there. Knocking on the door with the briefcase in his hand, David said," I believe you may be looking for this."

The man grabbed the briefcase and walked to the back of the room. The police began questioning David as to where he found it, etc.

Then the policeman asked David if he knew what was in it. David nodded his head. Yes, he knew it was cash and a lot of it. A very happy man interrupted them with a relieved shout, "Yes and it is all there! $10,000 in cash for a business deal in the morning. The briefcase fell off my car roof where in my excitement, I forgot and drove off." The police officer looked at David and said, "A lot of folks would not turn in $10,000 in unmarked bills." In typical David fashion, he just shrugged and said that it wasn't his money, and he would hope that someone else would do the same for him.

David turned to go. "Wait," the owner declared. "I would like to give you a reward. I will give you 10 percent." When David was recounting the story to me about an hour later, I lost my breath. "Disneyland," I interrupted with a gasp.

"We can take the three boys to Disneyland." (This was 1987. A family of five could have a fantastic trip to Disneyland for $1000.)

"No," said a surprised David. "I refused the reward. I was just returning the briefcase to its rightful owner." I must admit. I grumbled.

I said that he was a better person than I. I *would* have accepted the reward so we could go to Disneyland. Nothing like a wife to put a guilt trip on an honest deed!

David, a little exasperated, continued with his story. The man, however, asked David what his favorite charity was. So, David named our church. With that, David turned back to the car and drove home with Derek. So, this ended his recounting the story.

On Christmas Eve, our church had a candlelight service and our minister said how the candlelight signified the light that the Savior brought to the world. He also said that we, as Christians, could sometimes shed a little of that light in the world. With this thought, he said that he was reminded of this light on that very afternoon. A man had arrived that Christmas Eve afternoon at our church with a $1000 donation. He told the minister that he wanted to give it to the church because of David's request that it be given to his favorite charity. The $1000 went to a much better use than a trip to Disneyland. It was a lovely and feel- good candlelight service. Unfortunately, we happened to miss it because we were driving to grandparents in Houston.

You are wondering. Wait a minute. Didn't I mention that we got to go to Disneyland? It was a God wink. Just two months later, David's company said they needed for him to fly to Anaheim on business. This was the first time they had business in California and to my knowledge, they never had business there again. When we checked, it just so happened that there was a strange airfare promotion going on. Due to a two for one airfare special (have you ever heard of airlines doing this?), we could fly with David to Anaheim with two free tickets. The company would naturally be paying for the hotel room on a business trip. It still gives me goosebumps. This timing could not have been coincidence. When David finished his work assignment, we thoroughly enjoyed a wonderful Wallyworld trip. Plus, we all tried our hands at the *boogie* board on the Pacific surf. David cut a few mean waves. We had that trip to Disneyland with God's sweet timing after the children and I had a quick lesson of honesty and doing the right thing. So often, God answers prayers before we even know what or how to pray them.

It doesn't always turn out that way, but this time was a happy ending lesson.

In the meantime, I have begun in 1987, something I always wanted to do. I've begun my Ph.D. (in Organizational Behavior of Human Resources) at The University of Texas at Austin. They have an extended program that meets once a month. If I leave on Friday at 5 AM from Fort Worth, I can drive to Austin by 8 AM. I attend classes all day on Friday and Saturday, departing at 4 PM on Saturday. I couldn't do it without David's help. He makes sure that the boys depart in carpool on Friday morning, he purchases Friday night pizza, he gets them to their games on Saturday morning, and voila! I'm home for dinner on Saturday. This has been complicated by the fact that I have just begun working full time for General Dynamics. Until now we have not been a two-partner family income, but the attraction of insurance for potential three sets of dental braces plus the need to start saving for three sets of future college tuitions has made this job for me at General Dynamics very attractive. So, I work the forty hours Monday through Thursday at General Dynamics and leave for classes on Friday and Saturday. It's a two-year program of classes plus a year of dissertation. It's doable.

Now let's check on Eileen whose family has found out what their new adventure will be! They have moved to California for a year to attend language school. This will prepare them for an assignment to the Embassy in Rome.

From Eileen: Cara Amici, Buon Natale! Our Christmas greetings come from the beautiful Monterey Peninsula in California, home of the sea otter, monarch butterfly and the Defense Language Institute, where we are studying Italian. Next year Joe will be working with the Italian Ministry of Defense in Rome.

Learning Italian has been our full-time job since September. "Full time" is no exaggeration, as we spend 8 hours a day in class and have at least 3 hours of homework each night. There are only 9 students in the class, so it's impossible to be invisible—especially since our instructors are old pros at catching the unprepared! Joe's accent is . . indescribable—a cross between Napolitano, Sicilian and Brooklynese! My main problem has been thinking I am speaking Italian as Spanish rushes from my mouth.

After many years in aviation, Joe is just turning 40 and has substantial hearing loss which makes auditory learning difficult. Add to that, as Senior Officer at the school, Joe was often called away from the classroom to do Army business.

Joe was called away just as the instructor announced we would be studying "curses" because it was important to know if you were being insulted. Unbeknown to Joe, we postponed the subject which the instructor didn't feel comfortable teaching, to cover a unit on gardening. Joe quickly dashed back to the class as the instructor was saying "Cespuli"-bushes. She continued with the rest of the lesson while Joe madly tried to catch up by scribbling notes. She asked in her ladylike tone at the end if there were any questions. Joe raised his hand. "Sorry, I just want to clarify—was that Cespuli for bullshit?" Swallowing her tongue, this Victorian lady was aghast that anyone would say that word in her presence or think she was teaching that word. The lesson on curses came much later with a different male instructor. Bushes is now our favorite curse word.

The children are doing well and have made a great adjustment to the long hours. <u>Now,</u> they are the ones coming to check on <u>us</u> as we do our homework. Role reversal! Brett (at 12 going on 13) has flirted with football and is active in Boy Scouts, working toward Star Scout. Brigid at 16 has "found a home in the theatre." She both acted and was assistant director for the school's recent production of "Fools." She enjoys the atmosphere of the Pacific Grove High School and the activities of our church's Youth Group such as the dances and ski trips to Lake Tahoe. Even our eccentric dog, Harry, seems to thrive in this California climate . . .as do his fleas.

Our "new/old" house is in Pacific Grove-midway between Monterey and Carmel (of Mayor Clint Eastwood's fame). We're about a block from the bay and can hear the seals barking at daybreak. The house is almost 100 years old—complete with stained glass, high ceilings, chandeliers, and inadequate plumbing, antiquated dangerous electrical wiring and early on, we discovered MICE. Joe has the situation well in hand and we're quite civilized—if a bit primitive. Our only source of heat is the fireplace in the living room. We're praying that "sunny" California stays sunny at least until April. We were warned by the electrician that turning on the furnace would be equivalent to crossing the beams in "Ghost Busters". Or simply catastrophic. So, we paid attention.

We'll arrive in Rome around mid-May and have already received pictures of our apartment which is 5 kilometers north of the Vatican. To say we are excited is putting it mildly. So, all we want for Christmas is to pass our orals with flying colors!

Let's Discuss:

Music drifts into our consciousness at Christmas. Whether it is Adeste Fidelis (in Latin) that they are singing in Italy or Come Let us Adore Him in the United States, music brings us back to the season

. "Come Let us Adore Him…" That is a great invitation for your Christmas this year in the present.

Have you ever really stopped to think about these words of a song that we repeat so many times at Christmas? Third verse, "Yea, Lord, we greet thee. Born this happy morning. Jesus to Thee be all Glory given. Word of the Father. Now in flesh appearing." And then the Chorus, "O Come let us adore him." This is not hard. Are we ready for "Yea, Lord, we greet thee? "

On closer examination, isn't that what the Bible is all about? It is a Love Story. The next words ring out to us. The Father gave us the Word. (And we didn't quite get it.) So, The Word now became flesh, talking to us in the flesh as the Son of Man and the Son of

God. Angels greet him and celebrate him even to the end of his earthly life. We are only asked to appreciate God and give Him the glory of our appreciation. He is there for us. He is bringing the light into the world.

Ephesians 1:18-19 I pray also that the eyes of your heart may be enlightened in order that you may know the hope to which he has called you, the riches of his glorious inheritance in the saints and his incomparably great power for us who believe.

Let's Talk

1) What are your favorite Christmas hymns? Do you know the favorite Christmas hymns of each member of your family?

2) Have you truly examined the words of your favorite Christmas hymns lately?

3) Play them over in your mind, maybe one hymn a day. What do the words really mean? Or examine one hymn a week until Christmas as you drive. Maybe this way your heart can be enlightened so you may know the hope to which he has called you.

Christmas Countdown, 1988

1988 brings highs and lows of the Summer Olympics in Seoul, the launch of the Discovery Shuttle (since there has been a two and half year shut down following the Challenger disaster), and the loss of the Pan Am airplane due to a bombing over Lockerbie, Scotland.

From Brenda: For me there is the realization that we are reaching the end of the decade and it has been ten years since I had our last baby. I find so often that I want to snatch moments in time. How about you? Sometimes, do you want to put your foot on the brake and just capture a moment? If I freeze shot 1988, it would look like this.

If you picture my sons in technicolor, picture Derek at 13 with a turned-up brim red hat. He is a "skater" with the skateboard we bought last Christmas. Somehow David figured out how to build a 3' skateboard ramp that looks terrifying to me, but the boys can zip, zoom and "ollie" on it. Derek tried zipping and jumping over a manmade hurdle with his bicycle and skinned a large hunk of his side. Sneakily, he tried not to show me as he limped in to wash the blood away. There is more to that tale that my sons know, but a mom doesn't get to hear.

Remember that "no go cart" statement last year? Vance in the fourth grade loves to build things, so he worked on a push mobile of his own design with David. They will use it in a Scout push mobile race. No zipping and dashing since there is no motor. David is still Cubmaster of the local troop with 8 dens clamoring for his attention. Vance is the last of our cub scouts. Maybe David will get to hang up that uniform, yet!

Along with the rest of middle America we bought a Plymouth Voyager this year. It is the new and modern answer to a station wagon or a forerunner to the Suburban with a sliding side door. It was partially purchased because of my drive back and forth to Austin as I work on my graduate classes. But it was also purchased so each boy could have his own seat in the car. With this car, we do not have to draw imaginary lines, so each boy stays on his own side of the seat. Sometimes the back seat is full of quiet but fierce hand battles between them. Sometimes it is loud complaints requiring referees. David remarked that we pay quite a price just to have a little peace and quiet on the way to church. Sometimes that sliding door gets tricky. To the boys' humiliation, the door fell off while I was driving car pool. I still have no idea how it got off its track and spun to the dirt. I just picked it up, tossed it in the back and we continued via open air to get to school. They wanted me to park a block away and let them out. I told them to imagine our van was a convertible on its side. Amazing how a mom can embarrass her sons without really trying.

Fortunately, Justin has made the transition successfully to middle school. He has made it so successfully he wants his own phone line.

The answer is no. That will be interesting to see how the three boys will juggle the use of our one land line phone.

Now let's check on Eileen who says" Buon Natale e Felice Annon Nuova! It was Greetings from Rome.

This is our first Christmas in the "Eternal City." We are trying to combine elements of the American traditional holiday with the magic of the Italian holiday to include Midnight Mass at the Vatican with the Pope . . .and a few thousand of his most intimate friends.

We're slightly more than just tourists now, having spent the last few months getting settled in and adjusting to the differences between what we thought it would be like-charming, old world and romantic—with what it is really like. Frustratingly slow, outdated and crumbling. Reality lies somewhere between the two. We are experiencing a love hate relationship with Italy. Love for the people, their food, their warmth, and the amazing Italian culture. Frustration when we can't get things done until domani—the mythical tomorrow that is always promised but rarely delivered. All in all, we are delighted to being here, constantly looking forward to domani.

Joe loves his new job as the Chief Liaison Officer between US Military and the Italian military. He has been adopted by his Italian fellow officers. He is now truly Roman from the way he drives, sometimes creating his own lane, to his very strong morning espresso coffee in the local bar. We are fortunate to have found such wonderful friends. He has also taken on another labor of love, or of Hercules, by becoming the American Boy Scout Master of Rome. That is quite a title. He and Brett are usually knee deep in plans for the next hike or camp out.

Speaking of Brett, now 13, is busy with school and sports and keeps us all amused and amazed with his Italian. His crowning triumph came when we sent him to the store for six eggs and some cold cuts.

He came home with 6 grapes and raw turkey. Maybe it is hereditary.

Brigid is in her junior year, and it is her busiest ever. She is a bit of a pioneer attending Notre Dame International School being one of fifteen girls amid one hundred fifty boys in their first co-ed year. It is Heaven for a sixteen-year-old and hell for her parents. She has also joined their first volleyball team and is now into cheerleading—some things even feminists can't change.

I am now a new employee of the Italian Ministry of Defense. I'm teaching English to Field grade Army Officers in their equivalent of the War College. Finding the job was a stroke of luck probably caused by hundreds of candles lit by my mother. She nearly burned down Upstate New York, but I found work. It's work I love, and the people are wonderful. Can't ask for more than that.

For Eileen there has been an exciting move to Rome. For Brenda there is the realization that she is reaching the end of the decade and ten years since she had her last baby. Both Eileen and Brenda have mentioned that they would like to snatch moments in time. How about you? Do you sometimes want to put your foot on the brake and just capture a moment?

Let's Talk!

We want to describe these moments of Christmas and linger over them because we know how easily moments move to the corner of our memory.

We become so engrossed in living each day that we take for granted that we'll always know how a moment feels. Whether it is the crying of an infant in the night, the fresh skin smell of a six-month-old splashing in the bath, the accomplishments of first toddling steps when they let go of your hand, or the first time you notice your toddler's face is now that of a child, the memory is fleeting. From the first day of kindergarten or the proud glance of your child in the swimming pool as they learn not to fear the water, the moment flees. These moments are so tangible. Then time moves on and the children are in a new stage with a new normal and the former stage slips to the corner of our mind.

A memory can be taken out and dusted off with a photo album, but somehow a photo is missing the sensory dimension. It is partially for this reason that we have journaled through the years and wanted to write this book. In this way, we could give our children (and our friends) some thoughts and glimpses of growing up years. And in the case of senility, Eileen and I are hoping it will help us recognize ourselves.

1) Since Christmas is such a busy time, what plans have you made to capture these special moments? What are some ways to capture these?

2) Could a New Year's resolution be to journal, even if it is only small written phrases to jog the memories? Have you journaled? If not a written journal, do you have a photo journal? What if you put a journal book out for each person to write a Christmas wish or thought? Then each year this journal is brought out to add to the journal both as a keepsake and "living" addition each year?

3) Have you found yourself putting off until tomorrow (domoni) some true joy that you should do today? What is a

true joy that you need to expand while diminishing some of the "chores"?

4) Have you caught yourself in a compare and despair mode? Are you looking at others to see how their Christmas looks "all together" while yours is lacking? Are you savoring the good smells and sights of Christmas or focusing on what is lacking or how you feel you are lacking?

Christmas Countdown, 1989

From Brenda: “A yorkie,” I said, slightly aghast as Vance focused his big blue eyes on me in a pleading way. “Yeah, a really cute little puppy for Christmas, “he repeated while pushing his straw blond hair out of his eyes. Justin, standing next to me and almost as tall as me, said, “I’d like a Yorkie puppy, too. But I want one all to myself that could sleep on the end of my bed at night.” This brought a deep throated chuckle to Derek, who now is taller than I am. He patted me on the back in a consoling manner. “I guess that means I’ll have to ask for a German Shepherd puppy for Christmas, so it can eat up the Yorkie. “

David, sitting close by and in shock, asked the obvious question . . .”and who is going to feed and take care of this dog?” Naturally, both boys nodded their heads that **they** would meet every whim of such an adorable dog.

Why is it that as parents we can only see the mess and headache while visions of sugar plums are dancing in the heads of our youth?

What is the moment that we step from being a cheerful, well-balanced human being into the state of a grumpy old parent? We already had one dog, a two-year-old Sheltie. Unfortunately, the Sheltie bonded with me (who fed her) instead of the boys. She is my shadow. If I stopped quickly, she would run into me. So, how did we solve this dilemma?...

Sshh, don't tell but their Aunt Debbie is going to give the boys a Yorkie puppy for Christmas. (Her idea. The yorkie just happened to pop up via a friend whose dog just had puppies—what a coincidence). We'll name him Nikki for St. Nicholas. Hmmm, I'll have to think long and hard about how I can repay her kindness!!

So this is how Christmas, 1989 is going at our house. Derek has entered Ninth grade which is High School in Fort Worth. His high school has 3000 students. Derek seems undaunted by the school size. He is looking forward to "drivers' education" next Spring. Somehow David and I do not think the world is ready for Derek behind the wheel, so we are dragging our feet. Derek is enjoying doing some camera work at church and is interested in film work for a career. It will be interesting to see if this is also a passing fancy, but on Sundays, he is manning a camera for church.

Justin dreaded going back to 7th grade in his Middle School. All summer he fantasized about returning to elementary school. To add insult to injury, the day before school started, he dived into my parent's pool and knocked out a front tooth. Fortunately, his braces helped a little. A wild drive to the dentist office with the knocked-out tooth in a cup of milk ensued. The tooth was replaced, and the skinned-up face turned into multiple scabs. Therefore, he got to start his first day of 7th grade with a bloody scraped nose, fat lips but teeth intact and shiny with braces. I assured him with a mother's love (and small gulp) that he looked just fine.

Somehow the sympathy vote kicked in. The phone has been ringing off the hook with 7th grade girls, so I've noticed an attitude change. Seventh grade is looking better.

Vance still enjoys building things. He is in the 5th grade. He and David built a wooden model airplane with hundreds of small pieces. It took most of the summer to complete it. It flies but Vance is thinking bigger and better. He would like a plane with a motor or a remote-control car as his next project. He is at the age that he spends the night on the weekend with different friends for a sleep over. There is no way we can catch up with individual sleepovers, so we must have five or six Fifth graders to spend the night to repay the hospitality. There are always one or two boys in the bunch who do not seem to tire out. How can they sit there with wide open eyes almost all night long? Justin, on the other hand, does not like spending the night elsewhere, so his friends need to come here. Are you getting the picture of a room full of bedrolls? Then picture David and I rotating to visit the room to make sure that the bed count is still valid.

OK. Here is an update on Nikki. Vance said he gagged three times as he had to clean up "dog do. "He said that Justin wasn't holding up his end of the bargain. Vance thought maybe we should sell Nikki. By 9 AM when we were having breakfast and the boys were playing with Nikki, he said he guessed he'd only buy the dog back. As I am writing, it is night and Nikki is asleep on the waterbed with Vance. I think they have bonded. Nikki is stinky, but safe.

Here comes Eileen! Holiday greetings from the Eternal City! As we approach the Christmas season, we can't help but think that some capricious spirit has put our lives on FAST FORWARD. Is it possible that a year has gone by so quickly?

We need to treasure every minute of our tour here because it obviously agrees with us. This year has brought us many special events. Brett made his Confirmation in the Vatican at the Governor's Chapel. In fact, we had to wait with the Swiss guard at the gate because the Pope was strolling in the gardens. This was a graduation year for Brett as well. The highlight of his graduation ceremony was when he received the award for the most improved student in Italian from the Italian department. The change in his Italian accent and conversational ability in a year's time is amazing. He offered to translate for his father when they were on the street talking to a neighbor. Joe wisely accepted. He is now a Freshman in High School, so we are sure our lives are on fast forward.

Brigid spent a lot of time and energy working on "school spirit." If scholarships are available for that commodity, when she graduates this June, she'll get a free education. Most of her thoughts now center on college applications, SATs and figuring out a way to parlay her expanding language skills—English, Italian and German into a college major. If anyone can do it, she can.

Joe stays busy with his logistics activities working with the Italian Defense General Staff and EUCOM (European Command). We visited Heidelberg this Fall as part of a joint meeting held for the US/Italian military planners. He is blessed with wonderful folks in the Italian ministry who will be sorely missed when this chapter of our lives is over.

Eileen was given a full Italian government contract this Fall and is teaching at the Headquarters of the Italian Ministry Defense School of Languages. Somebody up there likes her a lot. She has the only authorized US only position in the Italian government. Her only complaint is that they keep "misplacing" the necessary documents to pay her salary.

Over the summer Brigid and Brett went for an infusion of "mall" and visited their grandparents in the States. We had planned to go on Safari to Kenya and Somalia, visiting friends there for a few weeks. A funny thing happened a day before we went to pick up the tickets. There was a small revolution in the capitol of Somalia, a few blocks away from our host's house. We made a minor change in our plans and went to Ireland instead. It was a great vacation. Beautiful sights. Friendly people. And the added possibility of looking up our ancestors. Or as Joe calls it, "chasing our ghosts." Maybe the "climate" will be friendlier with no revolutions in Africa next year.

Let's Talk

1) What part of your story has made you wonder, "God, are you really there? Are you really loving?"

2) When you were in that season of questioning God (or perhaps you are now), how did you see God at work in and around you – even if it didn't yield the results you were hoping for?

3) How can you interpret your current circumstances through God's goodness (rather than allowing your circumstances to interpret God's goodness)?

4) How can you put the brakes on FAST FORWARD? Sometimes this pace becomes an autopilot where you have no peace but push. "The Flourish Factor" by Courtney

Pinkerton offers some formulas for establishing a more vibrant and sustainable pace to remain resilient.

Brenda & David are visited by Joe & Eileen in Fort Worth, Texas

Christmas Countdown, 1990

Conversations overheard as Brenda writes this letter:

"I don't know, Justin, does this shirt look good?"

You know what that means—long penetrating gazes in the mirror to discern if the hair is curving to just the right angle and if a shirt is deemed "cool" by a wiser 8th grade brother. This means Vance's entire closet of hand-me-downs is suspect and leaning towards "uncool" as he braves Middle School and the 6th grade.

On the first day of Middle School, Vance told me to tell the teacher he had chicken pox, so he'd have to miss the first week. On second thought, he said, maybe the first semester. Justin quickly informed him that a backpack is not cool. Justin had carefully folded his notebook paper and pen into his pocket, so he is prepared for notes, but does not look prepared. That is the key—one must look casual as you stroll into school, but you are secretly prepared. Vance also wanted an individual "first day of school" picture with his dad so he could prove how much he had grown. When we arrived at school, Vance's friends walked up. Together, they approached the school door in a pack, walking very, very close together. They nervously eyed the nearby packed circles of giggling girls. The school bell clanged, and the concentric circles moved and merged. So far, so good.

"Well, let's see. I figure it's three months, six days and two hours."—that's Derek on the phone, in the 10th grade, who's become a mathematical whiz, giving up-to-the-minute calculations for when he turns 16 and can drive a car. This summer we took a family vacation to Yellowstone and Derek "practiced" his beginner's license by driving more than 60% of the time. Actually, he is a good driver leaving very few startled moose in his path—just a few clinched and white knuckled parents who smile and nod at his progress.

"Don't worry, Mom. I play the "left out" position—that's Justin, our 90 lb. 8th grader playing contact football against 150 lb. monstrous players. (For your information: Whenever the hulks shifted to the right, Justin ran to the left to catch a ball. He said just knowing what it felt like to be tackled added to his speed, and if it really got bad, a merciful coach "left him out" on the bench. Fortunately, he ended the season with the all-important letter jacket and no injuries.) I think in high school he may stick to golf and baseball. Vance, naturally, says he can't wait to play football next year.

Unfortunately, Justin had followed my advice in 8th grade Cotillion. I had noticed one curly-haired girl was not being asked to dance. I knew that Justin was well-liked, and my heart went out to the girl. So I suggested that at the next cotillion Justin should set the pace and ask her for the first dance which might encourage other guys to ask her to dance. Kindly and boldly at the next Cotillion dance, he strode across the floor and stopped directly in front of her. She jumped back as if burned by hot water. He repeated the question, "Would you like to dance? "And extended his hand. Words escaped her. She could only nod yes with a dazed look and followed him to the floor. Justin felt good. She felt good. I was proud of him. Unfortunately, she became obsessed. She soon began calling him, writing him notes, accidentally bumping into him in the hall. Even worse, her friends became equally obsessed and now he was being stalked in the halls by a moving pack of several of her friends. It was a small herd of girls that pursued him from class to class. He felt bummed by my advice for his 8th grade Cotillion class. Once again, I learned the hard way not to upset the ecological system of Middle Schoolers.

And from David, "Sure, Vance. The presents are hidden in the closet. Go ahead." That's really being a spoilsport. Now the boys can't pretend that they haven't searched out the hiding place and unwrapped then carefully rewrapped the Christmas packages. By placing the responsibility firmly on their shoulders for the "surprise" element and giving them the choice, David is weighing them with a heavy burden. Then David looks at me and winks— "Do you think we can have Christmas in February—maybe by then we'll have everything finished."

In the meantime, my conversation is a mumble. I am in the dissertation doldrums—trying to get my committee to agree on the chapters I am writing for my doctorate at the University of Texas at Austin. Since I was selected for Leadership Texas, a women's leadership networking program, I decided to use this group of 90 Texas leadership women for my dissertation on Leadership

Development. It has been a wonderful opportunity and I'm still in the challenge of it all.

Merry Christmas from Eileen. Once again, we send our greetings and the best of wishes from Rome. This will be our last Christmas here but we're still not sure where next year will find us. Watch for our change of address with next year's wishes.

We've experienced our shares of highs and lows this year. Brigid graduated from Notre Dame International in June. It was great to have Mom and Dad Buchheit here to share the excitement of graduation week with us while they had their Roman holiday. Brigid began her studies at the University of Maryland in Munich, Germany. We were especially proud of her accomplishments in language starting her college career with 9 credit hours thanks to advanced placement classes at NDI. She held a full-time job this summer at the embassy and took a summer school class in Italian at night. In Germany she continued to pursue her advocation in acting and enjoyed a role in Thurber Carnival this November—wonder where she got that touch of ham from!

Brett did himself proud by receiving his letter in wrestling in his freshman year. This was quite an accomplishment, especially at NDI. He is still active in Boy Scouts. This year he is the Senior Patrol Leader for the troop. For summer camp the troop went to High Adventure training in Germany and as a special treat for Brett's 16th birthday, he threw himself off the Alps while learning the fine art of repelling with a Canadian Airborne unit. All of this was much to Eileen's chagrin. We changed apartments within days of the Scouters return so they escaped the "Oh, God, we're moving panic." (If Eileen had known what Brett was doing, it would have been more than chagrin.)

Among our Low's was the death of Eileen's father shortly before Christmas last year. He had suffered a long debilitating illness but fought it to the end. "Nana Nurse" was coerced into a visit to us in the Spring. She liked it so much that she came back in the Fall along with Eileen's brother. Now she is an honorary Roman.

Also, Eileen and Brigid were invited to a concert at the South African Embassy. Midway through the performance the Ambassador received the news that Nelson Mandela would be released the next day. To be in the South African embassy when this announcement was made was like touching history.

Let's Discuss!

Americans live to work, but Italians work to live. The culture shock for Joe and Eileen was to adjust from the laid back Domani style to return to frenetic America. Joe and Eileen began to question the sanity of constant frenetic activity. Americans prize productivity and the ability to "get er done". Suddenly Joe and Eileen questioned, was something being lost in constantly trying to prove our worth?

At Christmas we can be reminded of a world of unconditional love or grace. That door is opened to everyone. We don't have to prove our worth. "Give thanks to the Lord, for he is good. His faithful love endures forever." Psalm 107:1

1) Have you heard these conversations this week? "It's just so busy, everyone's so busy. Kids, school, work, moving houses, so who has time?" What is your answer? Is it, "if I don't do it, it won't get done?" Can you delegate or lessen the burdens?

2) Are you caught in the more is better mentality of gift giving? Are you caught in the strain of trying to "equalize" the gifts?

Are you weighed under the burden of paying for the gifts you have bought on credit? What are some options?

3) Have you, too, given well-meaning advice to your children only to have it backfire on you? For example, the Middle School stalking by a gaggle of giggling girls on unsuspecting and quiet Justin? Can you think of some examples?

Christmas Countdown, 1991

From Brenda: The smell right now on this Saturday afternoon is chocolate chip cookies. Vance just decided to bake a batch of cookies from scratch. They smell great. But when we take a bite, there's something missing to their taste. We then discovered the brown sugar still sitting on the counter. Vance is a little disgusted, but as David observed, at least it got Vance talking to us while he worked. Most conversations about 7th grade are monosyllabic. At 5'6" he's a busy socialite, lettering in the current sport, making excellent grades, and borrowing the clothes of his older brothers.

There is also the smell of cinnamon in the air. The youth group from church made our home one of its stops last night in a progressive dinner. Nothing like 50 kids coming to your house to speed your Christmas decoration action. I learned that cinnamon and a few strategic candles really add to the atmosphere since our baking isn't always a success. This same youth choir group is going to Canada next summer and will be a guest of the Montreal Expos. This is a terrific opportunity for my two high school sons, Justin, and Derek. Justin, now a 5'7" ninth grader, has adjusted well to his first year in high school, strong in academics and the sports he loves. He has now narrowed down the sports that he plays to baseball, golf and church basketball. Girls are not a major item. Derek, on the other hand, merely tolerated his junior year. Basically, school aggravates him. He is now 6' tall. This last week he discovered his latest interest is junior boxing. His real interest was getting a car last March. His granddad gave him a 1977 Impala, worth $1200 and we then put $1500 in repair. The horn went out, the lights went out and it refused to start. But it has lots of heavy metal to protect Derek. Unfortunately, this protection was proven to be needed as he had an accident on July 4th,. He made it three months without an accident. We decided to sell the car. We got $350. Then he had a minor wreck in our car. He is now saving his money for his next car. Most of our driving time is spent getting the three sons to diverse sports activities.

I asked David what his favorite sport is. He said it's running down the hall to jump in bed and read his newspaper in peace and quiet. We make sure he gets his exercise, though. He now walks 2 dogs as he jogs nightly, but so far, he refuses to include the puppy. (Yes, Vance got our 3rd dog which he purchased with his own money and plans to breed—an English Jack Russel terrier named Robin. She is named after Robin Hood). We can foresee the boys leaving for college and we will be walking a string of pulling, yelping, sniffing old dogs who have begged us with pleading eyes to be taken on daily walks. David also expressed his artistic talent by designing a patio outside our back door. This required his setting 1,650 bricks in a brilliant herring bone diagonal pattern. He was doing great until Vance decided it needed to be finished in time for a 13th birthday boy/girl party dance. . .on the new patio. The bricks did fly, still trembling in place when the first guest arrived. Vance also got a birthday camouflage/paint gun party out of the deal since his cousin Austin was visiting from Washington, D.C.

My big project is "phinally "done. On December 8, I walked across the stage in cap and burnt orange hooded gown for U.T., Austin. My parents, husband and three sons were there with cheers and tears of their own. David was present at my final defense for my dissertation, having helped me with the last-minute perfect margins, table, and millions of completed details to get the dissertation bound. When my committee said, "Congratulations, Dr. Shull," I immediately looked to David to see a mirrored tear in his eye. On the way out the door, he gave me a shove and said, "Dr. Shull, is that a foot powder?" The boys asked if the carpool had to call me Dr. Mom. Then, yesterday when I called Justin by the wrong son's name, I told him that it's terrible to get my doctorate just in time to lose my mind. I never seem to get the boys 'names recalled in the correct order at the correct disciplining moment. I just run down the alphabet until I get to the correct kid. I wonder. Is that approaching age or approaching Christmas crazies?

I have been working as a management consultant in Dallas-based firms. This means a 45-minute commute of kamikaze tactics from Fort Worth to Dallas. That, too, breaks down the brain cells. The good news is that the Dallas office is in the towers of the Galleria of Dallas. This is a major mall with a skating rink. That certainly makes Christmas shopping too easy to pop downstairs on lunch break. The pocketbook shudders!

Eileen, on the other hand, admits that she is suffering culture shock in reverse.

It all began with my trip back to the United States to buy a house in our old neighborhood of Chesterfield, Missouri. Friends of ours at the Embassy have a son living in Chesterfield. They gave me a key to his apartment because he would be away the week I came to the states. Our realtor was an old friend from our previous assignment there in Chesterfield. She and her husband picked me up at the airport and drove me to the apartment. We unlocked the door and a wall of cat odor hit us in the face. A litter box had never been changed and the dust and dirt swished us in the face. The sweet couple said, "You can't stay here." But I assured them it would be ok. They insisted on emptying the litter box and taking out the trash before they left. Being severely jet lagged, all I wanted was a shower and to sleep. I went into the bathroom and realized I would not be able to have those towels touch my body. So, I took a shower and air dried. The bedding unfortunately was as bad as the towels. I dressed again and laid on top of the bedspread. Sometime around dawn I thought I was having a heart attack. There was a heaviness in my chest. I opened my eyes to discover a face in my face. It was a cat who had been in that apartment for a week alone. I called my realtor friends and said, "I give." They took me to a nearby motel and I surrendered the key and the cat to well -meaning neighbors.

We knew the real estate was stable, the schools were excellent, and that Joe would retire following this assignment so buying a house in Chesterfield was a no brainer. After seeing many houses, I made my choice, and we went to the bank to get a mortgage. I handed my charge card to the banker and said, "put it on this." He said, "We've never done that before." I countered, "There's a first time for everything." And it worked. I charged it on my credit card. Before I left St. Louis, I visited old friends at St. Louis University, and they gave me my old job back.

Back to Rome for farewells and packing, I got a pass for a special store called Metro similar to Costco. I bought cases of pasta and cheese that we would find difficult to get in America. When the movers came to our apartment, they looked at the cases and said, "Lady, they got no food in America?"

Once back in Chesterfield, old friendships were resumed. Brett and Chris Kohunsky, his buddy since 3rd grade picked up where they left off. My friends welcomed me back at SLU. Joe went back to familiar faces at AVSCOM (Aviation Systems Command). Brigid opted for a change. She chose to go to SUNY (State University of New York) Stonybrook near her Uncle Joe. This is supposed to be our last move!

Let's Talk!

Eileen at last was finding some stability from multiple moves and Brenda had finished a long journey of achieving her doctorate and volunteerism. But it was time to reconsider. In all the times of saying" Yes, I can do that," were we in danger of having said no to family listening time, quality time with spouse, siblings, friends, or God? Quality time of deep and slow connection would help us to remain grounded.

1) Have all your yeses in this holiday crunch resulted in saying no to family (spouse, children, siblings, friends or God) quality time?

2) Do you have friends, relatives or employees who can help you, so you are less clogged with expectations and freer with grounded listening? Can you delegate some of your tasks?

3) Have you tried lately to listen more and" do" less in this holiday? What would it look like if you tried listening more and doing less by striking some things off your calendar?

4) When Mary and Elizabeth came together for the first and last time in the Gospels (Luke 1:39-40), two "lowly people" had been chosen and blessed by God. Both are carrying a child of destiny—Elizabeth with John the Baptist, and Mary with Jesus. Only kind words are spoken to each other. There is a stillness and goodness here that is unlike so many other Gospel scenes of conflict and hostility. God's presence floods their hearts like sunlight floods a room. We need those moments of stillness, kindness, moments of prayer, where the peace of Christ is present. Have you taken the time to communicate with another Christian where you both have Christ within you? You have a bond that is far more important than all that might divide you. It is then that God floods your heart like sunshine. Are you ready for some "Sonshine?"

Christmas Countdown, 1992

From Brenda: This year I decided to update you with a mental picture of the family. That way you can see for yourself:

1. The boys are 14, 15 and 17 and yes, all are almost taller than David.
2. David still has a flat stomach. (He held it in for the picture.)
3. Yes, I'm looking older, but those are padded shoulders on my sweater—it's the fashion these days. I look much thinner and younger in person. Really?

Derek is a senior in high school. We found West Academy which has a flexible curriculum and school hours. He is looking forward to FREEDOM (his 18th birthday) when he believes the world will acknowledge his adulthood. The open roads beckon, beautiful babes will adore him, and school/studying will be limited to an undecided college course or maybe not. The rubber meets the road in '93. We try to tell him that being on your own isn't all he thinks. It has been a hard year for him and us as he works toward adult freedom.

Justin is the proud owner of new/only 6 years old '86 jeep Cherokee. We found this great deal in Tulsa, Oklahoma while I was on a consulting assignment. Justin flew up to join me and we drove it home. One problem. It is a stick shift, not automatic. It was "on the job" learning. Up close and personal. Grinding and bumping our way to Dallas, he got the hang of it after 100 miles or so. Remember how tough shifting can be as you start up a car at a stop light? This is a little terrifying for the driver and for the front seat passenger with plastered smile who is surreptitiously mashing the passenger floorboard. Out of the corner of his eye, I think he caught me mashing the floorboard. Fortunately, once out of the city, it was smooth sailing on the open road—no shifting and grinding gears.

When his younger brother asked for a ride home from school, Justin replied, "Vance, do you even KNOW how much gas that is?" He then instructed me to lock the car doors. Suddenly, he turned to me and gasped. "On no! That sounded just like Dad." I think he is out washing the car right now.

Vance is the proud owner of four puppies. His Jack Russel terrier was bred. He couldn't settle for a local stud. We had to drive two hours for the perfect one, but the results are adorable (but to be sold). This is his money-making project and the first time I had witnessed the birth of puppies. We are not keeping any. Read my lips—no more dogs. I overheard him on the phone interviewing potential buyers. He asked if they had a yard, etc. as this energetic Jack Russell breed is not genetically wired for an apartment—even though it is the same dog as on the TV show Frazier which takes place in an apartment. When the prospective buyer replied, "no yard," Vance said," No thanks." He wouldn't sell. The prospective buyer said Vance couldn't do that. Vance replied he wanted the buyer to be happy with the right fit. He didn't want the dogs to be returned to the pound by unhappy owners. It seems like pretty good thinking to me from a 14-year-old. If you remember Nikki, our Christmas dog, we have an update. He remains an integral part of the family, loves sleeping with the boys or immediately jumping in the lap of whomever sits down. Nikki has quite the personality. When you throw the ball, he waits for the other dogs to fetch it. He intercepts it at the very last moment going for the glory, not the work. He shows tremendous speed when you open the front door, ignoring voice commands, digging in with all fours to escape out the door and take himself on a walk.

David has gotten on the golf course a little more since he has golf partners in his sons. I have been travelling more as a management consultant and he has played a terrific Mr. Mom. His job still requires travel, but we have been able to juggle schedules.

This summer as a family (minus David who had to work), we went on a mission trip. We spent the week as guests on the Navajo reservation while our group produced a Vacation Bible School experience for the Navajo children. My sons were surprised by the lack of electricity, lack of running water and lack of indoor plumbing. The boys were joined by their cousin Austin from Washington, D.C. With bravado the four of them planned to camp out the first night in the dusty desert. As the night progressed, thoughts of desert snakes wriggling into bedrolls loomed larger and larger in their minds. Somehow, by sunrise all four boys were draped and jammed in a parked car. The tent was abandoned.

They also learned a new way to take showers. Showers now were taken in late afternoons because the hand drawn water had to warm up via the sun in overhead buckets. Then the buckets were pulled to plunge onto the victim below. No running water was a new experience for these city slickers.

There were lots of new experiences. While we were handing out flyers for the Vacation Bible School, we approached slowly and respectfully the homes of the Navajo in our car. Of course, the homes were far apart and the avalanche of dust behind our car was a dead giveaway to our approach. It was easy to spot us rolling toward their homes. This was no surprise attack. Vance learned, up close and personal, that some breeds of chickens can be very territorial and speedy. He politely delivered a flyer to a door with a Navajo family sitting on the porch. He invited the children to our Vacation Bible School. Then he raced madly back to the car with one chicken in close pursuit of him. I think the chicken won.

David's mother and dad flew in from Houston for Thanksgiving. At 89 years, David's dad navigates airports well and is giving Bob Hope competition for active living. Unfortunately, David's mom is being side lined more often due to Alzheimer's. My parents joined us and are doing well after a difficult spring due to a fluke accident in the airport for my dad. All is well, but it was a scary aneurism. This follows his earlier survival of non-Hodgkin's lymphoma at the age of 56. He has been in remission for twelve years now. We are happy that our parents are with us.

Remember I mentioned a planned trip to Canada that the youth choir group took? I will let Justin tell you about it.

"Here we were, all 34 of us, gazing at each other in disbelief! We were going to sing the National and Canadian anthems in the Skydome in Toronto. We stood watching 50,000 Canadians locate their seats. I watched in awe as Dave Stieb warmed up. Then I heard, "Mr. Bell, can I have your autograph?" Derek Bell was expected to get American League "Rookie of the Year" and he was standing just a few feet away. I frantically wanted to ask for an autograph, but wait a minute—no pen? Our director signaled for us to start our descent onto the playing field, heading to second base. We arranged ourselves into our lines and there was Derek Bell standing right there among the girls in the soprano section. Everybody's eyes in the stadium were glued to second base, including a chuckling Dave Winfield. The camera panned us and the big screen TV brought us close. Before we knew it, we were singing the last notes to "O Canada" and 50,000 people started to clap. I cannot describe the feeling of the roar of the fans. As we filed off the field, I saw none other than future Hall of Famer George Brett standing there clapping for us. I will never forget the big smile he gave me. Our fame was over in as much time as it had started, but for the moment a lot of Canada was watching us because of one man. Thank you, Mr. Bell."

This was quite a thrill for my son who lived, breathed, and now sang at a sports event.

From Eileen, it is a transition of becoming a civilian since Joe has decided to retire on Jan. 31st. This will be our last year in the military.

Eileen says, "Our move from Rome to St. Louis brought us back to the same neighborhood we had lived in before our European adventure. But now, it must be time to move again, because the last of the boxes have finally been stowed away and our near-term projects on our house are close to completion. That is much too settled for our blood. We are thinking that if we are lucky enough to stay in the St Louis area when Joe retires, we will build a deck to enjoy the summers. So, perhaps if you visit us this summer, bring a hammer.

In other news, Brett is enjoying "ruling" the school as a senior in Chesterfield West High School. He is knee deep in SAT, ACT and college applications looking for schools offering a major in commercial art and advertising. He has also discovered that driving is expensive—insurance, gas, upkeep and the like.

Brigid has changed majors and now has changed schools. She is taking classes in communication and human relations right here in Chesterfield, Missouri. Along with that she has turned into a grease monkey. Several months ago, a 1984 Mazda RX7 GSL-SE (limited production model) joined our family in less than running condition. Months later, the dents, sound system, suspension, and engine have been overhauled and it only needs a fresh paint job to look like new. This has been a father/daughter adventure. It's good to have her home with us again—when we see her.

Eileen is still teaching at St. Louis University in Orientation USA to acclimate foreign students to US colleges. Every semester brings a new crop of faces anxious to learn as much as possible—a teacher's dream! Joe's still muttering that between my job and his pension, he could work just 4 days a week at McDonald's and still be on the links 5 days a week. Keep dreaming!

The newest addition to our family is Chesapeake Bay Retriever named Lui-Louie. He's Louie for the language we left behind and the city we came to. This was Eileen's birthday present, and he's stolen all our hearts. Harry provides the training, so as you would guess, Louie is rapidly becoming a juvenile delinquent. We'll have no new furnishings for a while.

This has truly been a memorable year for us and may ring in the first location stability we have ever had. It has been 29 moves in 24 years!

Let's Talk!

The Magic of Christmas is not in the presents, but in His presence. As Brenda mentioned, her family went on their first mission trip to the Navajo nation. It was the first time she heard favorite hymns sung in Navajo.

Brenda says: You could feel His presence. Sitting in that little wooden church with windows open and a soft breeze from the desert, I heard stories from the native American Christians who had risked abuse from their families if they snuck away to church to worship. One woman told how her sister was beaten for attending church. Her sister would sneak to the end of the pasture with church clothes underneath her regular clothes and run to the church. Upon her return, her father beat her with jagged barbed wire. Yet this woman and that same father became a Christian. The quiet hymns in the Navajo church sung without a piano assured me of His presence.

The Navajo experience gave further contrast. We had created a Vacation Bible School in a large room that was the chief's headquarters. It was a culture shock to see women listening to our Bible stories while they worked on ancient looms. They were spinning the sheep wool for rugs, just as their ancestors had done for centuries. Yet, near them were people using their computers—a several hundred-year leap in one room.

1) Have you experienced His presence in unconventional sacred surroundings?

2) Have you sought out a church's chapel or a simple sacred place and begun your worship with silence? Have you attended a service where you didn't really understand a word of the language, but there was such warmth that no translation was necessary? What was that like?

3) Have you experienced God in light breaking over the mountains, or the quiet whisper of curtains wafting in the breeze of a church window? Isaiah 58:8 "Then your light shall break forth like the dawn and your healing shall spring

up quickly; your vindicator shall go before you and the glory of the Lord shall be your rear guard."

4) When has light broken over you to reveal his presence?

Christmas Countdown, 1993

From Brenda: Twas the night before Christmas and all through the house.

All *the creatures were stirring—this is the Shull house.*

David in his nightshirt with a gleam in his eye.

While I'm still wrapping presents with a sigh.

Vance hanging his stocking by the chimney with care.

At fifteen, he's either playing computer or on the phone with flair.

When out on the driveway, there arose a clatter.

It's Justin in his jeep, rushing to watch sports patter.

Meanwhile, what to our wondering eyes does appear.

But Derek back from Colorado—are those more girls calling I hear?

It's Christmas run amuck—no rest for the weary.

That's Christmas at our house—Doesn't it make you teary?

Now dash away, dash away. Christmas cards to all

We send our love and best wishes to each one of ya'll.

The rhythm's stinko and the rhyme's not quite true

But we think of you often and say Merry Christmas to you!

The pace may be hectic, but we wouldn't change a thing.

We're counting our blessings—Alleluia to sing!

Send us a card—let us hear your story

When all's said and done, to God be the glory!

From Eileen: This year brought major changes and yes, another move. This marked our 30th and hopefully last move which was made in June to Connecticut. Our new (and final!) home is an 1848 farmhouse called Fairview Farm in Bridgewater, Connecticut. It came complete with a sheep, a goat, several cats, assorted mice, and a 3-story barn. The sheep is an attack ram we call Kramer after the Seinfield character who is his kindred spirit. The goat is naughty—the previous owner's term. In goat behavior this translates into an escape artist who will eat anything while walking on top of cars. Our dogs herd them with glee. The rehab of the house is coming along nicely. Life on the farm is never dull. In addition to catching and returning the Houdini goat (the fire department, the police force and several town elders chip in). There is a small orchard with apple, pear and peach trees, a barn, shed, greenhouse, 2000 sq ft garden and 3 pastures to take care of. Joe is only a part time farmer, though, as his job at Sikorski keeps him busy Monday through Friday.

Joe is managing Sikorski's efforts to market its extensive depot capability to international customers. This is a new business direction for Sikorski and Joe is helping them break ground. Starting anything new is a challenge, but Joe is looking forward to having many Sikorski's around the world—not to mention the travel which Eileen hopes to share.

Eileen is on a sabbatical, the length of time directly related to rehab of the house and her desire to see it completed in this century. This has been a lifelong dream and there will be no rushing it along. Besides, there is the goat to catch.

Brett graduated from high school with his teachers cheering loudest of all in the audience, probably with relief. He is starting college at SW Missouri State University in Springfield, Missouri. The Kmart is the cultural center of the town. He's doing great and is now able to speak fluent Redneck in addition to Italian.

Brigid is completing her degree at Maryville University in Chesterfield rather than try 4 colleges in 4 years

As for the new year, January 24 will mark our 25th anniversary. Here's hoping we spend the next 25 at this address.

Let's Discuss!

Let's look at another hymn. O Holy Night! The stars are brightly shining. It is the night of the dear Savior's birth! Long lay the world in sin and error pining Till he appeared and the soul felt its worth. A thrill of hope the weary world rejoices For yonder breaks a new and glorious morn!

When Brenda was in the Fourth Grade, her teacher asked her and two others (Joyce and Tommy) to sing solo in a Christmas School program.

Brenda says: We each were given a verse and the class choirs would join us for the chorus. My solo part was: Til he appeared, and the soul felt its worth.

Now, as an adult, I realize what a key part that was.

Isn't that what we all want? Because He appeared, we could finally know our worth deep in our soul. There is Someone who loved and appreciated our worth.

1) Have you questioned whether you are loved and if anyone can appreciate your worth?

2) Are there times in life that cause that deep knowledge of appreciation to fade?

3) Have you experienced the loss of a parent? Even when you are an adult, the loss of a parent haunts your thinking for many years to come!

4) What helps you remember that you are loved and rekindles your belief in self and God?

5) There are graces that have come into our life—people who happen into our life at just the right time, insights that come out of the blue that are helpful, getting out of a jam by accident. Those are graces. It is all a gift from God. Have you experienced God's grace lately of forgiveness, good ideas, the power to do good works—all is a gift from God?

Christmas Countdown, 1994

From Brenda: David says it is a sign of the "emptying nest" syndrome, I couldn't get the flock together for a photo at Thanksgiving. Further signs of the time:

- Derek has returned from Colorado to take classes at the local junior college this year. It's the "No mon, no fun" predicament. Although he would prefer to be independently wealthy, he couldn't be at Thanksgiving dinner because he was working at his waiter job at Bennigan's.
- Vance, on the other hand, is a member of the jet set. He couldn't be at Thanksgiving dinner because he had a "great" chance to fly via private jet to the Texas/Baylor game with his good friend Nicholas. If he restricts his flying to a jet and not his car, I figured it was ok. He turned 16 and got a used car along with his driver's license. This means I no longer can eavesdrop during carpool to find out what REALLY is going on in the guy's life.

- Justin did join us for Thanksgiving (with my parents and sister's family—who are doing great). This, of course, was only a temporary lag in his social life of his senior year between football games and out with friends. Since he's a senior, we mostly hear the call of "See you later, Mom & Dad" and the vroom of his car exhaust. He is looking over colleges and is leaning toward The University of Texas at Austin. He has visited Georgetown University in D.C. but he rejected it because of no football games. He visited Vanderbilt but can't get U.T. Austin out of his mind. We naturally like the in- state tuition of U.T. He is slightly amazed that the same dorms are still standing from his dad and my college days there. He thought they had been razed by marauding dinosaurs.
- David's folks could not join us. David's dad celebrated his 91st birthday and his mom her 81st but they were recuperating from a flying trip to David's brother in Washington, D.C, no less.
- David on the other hand retains his five-minute commute to work. I know that's what keeps him looking so young. This was a banner year for him—just like a fine wine, he only gets better with age—at least that's what ARP said, when it welcomed him to the club on his 50th birthday! He feels aggravated that they invite young 50-year-olds to join, but then he likes the discounts. He felt he had to show off during a sand lot Volleyball game and limped with a twisted knee for the next few days. However, he assures me and the boys that he can arm wrestle with the best of them!

From Eileen:

This year has marked beginnings and endings for the Buchheits—some happy and some sad. Among the happy moments, we can count Brigid's graduation from Maryville

University! She is the happy recipient of a degree in Communications—something she'd always excelled at! After her internship last summer with Sikorsky, she has yearnings for things eastern, but the job market seems more attractive in the Midwest. Stay tuned for employment news!

- *Also on the plus side is Eileen's return to the work force. She has gone back to teaching ESL classes; this time it is Teikyo Post University in Waterbury. Most of her students are from Japan. The animals on the farm are pleased that her schedule allows sufficient time for their care and feeding. The group has increased to one old goat (not Joe), one ram, one ewe, two yearlings, a rooster, three barn cats, two dogs and the latest, three pygmy goats, two of which are pregnant. Joe may need another fob for the feed bill! These are also of the escape artist variety, so it's never dull.*

- *Brett continues to take on the world, getting a job as a mountain climbing instructor last summer—every mother's dream! He returned to SMSU in the Fall but plans to transfer to-- maybe Connecticut? He's been very active on campus, having articles published and submitting pieces for art shows. His grades have been gold, so we'll see where the next two years will take him.*
- *Joe's world travels increase and multiply as more and more nations decide they need helicopter depots. Now most of the near, middle, and far east is on his list of places to go and people to see. He is equally hard at work on the farm. He's now a pro at the construction of stone walls, paths, and repair/replacement of 150-year-old windows. The addition to the house has progressed at the same speed in which the sphinx was built, but Joe's chipping away at the "Job List," without the help of multitudes.*

- *Among the endings this year, we mourn the loss of Joe's mother, our beloved "Big Nana." She fought a brave fight against cancer and, typical of her, it looked like she'd win. Unfortunately, that terrible disease took over after a five-year battle. She showed us all how to look death in the face with courage and determination. She's sorely missed.*
- *As we come to the end of 1994, we think of all our friends, so spread out over this earth and the next. All our best wishes and the happiest of new years and the joy and blessings of the year to come!!*

Let's Talk!

Both Eileen and Brenda's family are now transitioning from child-filled Christmases. The expectation and meaning of Christmas change. It changes from being more children-oriented to more adult-oriented celebrations. As adults, we prepare Christmas for others through gift buying, party throwing, etc. It is a different anticipation.

1) Have you experienced an emptying nest at Christmas, or family members too far away to be together for Christmas? How have you handled the separation? Have you tried expanding your family to invite lonely neighbors or friends to your celebration to fill the spaces?

2) Have you worked with your family to do a service project at Christmas to expand the sense of family to strangers? Remember Ezra 4: "Rise up, take courage and do it."

3) Family life means new stages of development whether adding new members or losing family members. How has this affected you? How has this affected your Christmas celebration? What are some favorite examples of Christmas Past and Christmas Present? How can you combine the two?

Christmas Countdown, 1995

From Brenda: Imagine this historical (hysterical) photograph. We are in our favorite spot (Colorado) on the Ute trail, in the Colorado Rockies, on Brenda's birthday in July. Now here are what the four people in the photo are really thinking.

Justin—I leave for the University of Texas in just weeks, Freshman year, Freshman babes, freedom!

Brenda—I wonder if there is some way we can just stay in Colorado for all summer. I wonder if I can reinvent my second adulthood, leave my job and escape Justin's college tuition?

David—I wonder what Derek is doing to the house back in Ft Worth while we are on vacation here?

Vance—I get Justin's room, the phone alone—say, there may be a real advantage to being the only kid in the family left at home.

I can report. The house was fine, Justin's adjusting well to life at a big university and Vance is not so sure that having all this attention by both parents is such a good idea. It brings scrutiny, but he's holding up well for his junior year. We have maintained our sense of humor despite a transitional year of one more son leaving the nest.

From Eileen: Greetings again from beautiful Connecticut! Life on the farm continues to be:
full of adventures -- the never-ending renovation of "This Old House" and the comings and goings of our flock. Among the "goings" this year, we include ·"Kramer", the attack ram and his partner in crime, "Reggie", the musical rooster. They were in cahoots in an attack on Eileen, leaving her bruised, battered, and bloodied.

The next day found Reggie in the mulch pile and Kramer made into "ram-burger" for the local soup kitchen. There was peace in the pasture the following day, but the word was out-- "Don't hack off the food lady!"

Joe and our retired Navy friend, Jim Ducharme, have worked miracles on our 1848 treasure by replacing windowpanes, insulating walls, plaster boarding, painting and the like. The exterior has newly painted porches, fencing (a necessity on any farm with goats) and landscaping improvements throughout. And Eileen's list continues......

J oe keeps his "farmer" status alive and well in his off hours. The grounds are really looking good, and he has the satisfaction of driving his beloved tractor often. He even won a prize in the annual Tractor Parade held each Labor Day here in Bridgewater- something about "it's not the size of the tractor", etc.,

Joe continues to rack up his frequent flier miles. The last three months have been spent "commuting" between Madrid and JFK. Madrid is much preferred to Seoul, Korea and any place in Taiwan! Sikorsky hopes for his success in getting those foreign buyers!

Brigid made the move east last spring. After some false starts and disappointments, she found a great job with the advertising firm, Young and Rubicam. She's using her foreign languages and loves working in Manhattan. · She found an adorable apartment in Jersey City and finds the commute a snap on the PATH train. Her really big news is the announcement of her wedding next October! The future groom, Kemal Cengiz, was working on his master's in engineering when she was an undergraduate at Maryville. Right now, they have a long-distance relationship, as he is visiting his family in Turkey. Brigid has not met them yet.

Brett has made his transfer official. Starting in January, he'll be a UCONN junior. He's sporting a 4.0 GPA this semester in preparation for the transfer. He spent the summer doing an internship at the Grand Canyon. The experience of living in a remote outpost and having to carry in all his food was most profound. His appreciation of nature -- and groceries -- has· sharpened. This summer he'll be biking cross-country to raise money for AIDS research.

Let's Talk:

One of the favorite Christmas hymns is "Joy to the World." It is an overflowing of joy and anticipation, sung with energy! However, when Isaac Watts wrote this hymn, it was to describe and celebrate the second coming of Christ—not the first!

Most of us don't spend much time contemplating the second coming when Christ returns triumphantly to create a new heaven and a new earth. However, now that you know this, in the years to come, may you recapture the childlike joy of expectation—celebrating both Christ's first coming and eagerly anticipating the second coming!

"Then I looked and heard the voice of many angels, numbering thousands upon thousands and ten thousand times ten thousand. They encircled the throne and the living creatures and the elders. In a loud voice they sang: Worthy is the Lamb, who was slain, to receive power and wealth and wisdom and strength and honor and glory and praise." Revelation 5: 11-12.

1) With this new perspective about "Joy to the World" being Christ's triumphant return, do the words have a different meaning for you than they did before?

2) How does Advent/Christmas relate to our everyday experience of God and our expectation of Christ's return?

3) Reflect on the way that hymns tell the story of Jesus birth. Some are quiet like a lullaby, whereas others sound forth the joy of the angels. Do these fit the mood of the way you celebrate Christmas? Are your ears and heart open to the message of love that they bring us? Do you seek the quiet or rejoice in the constant surround sound of Christmas hymns?

Christmas Countdown, 1996

From Brenda:

Tis the Season of Christmas when all through the house

Things are a jumping, especially my spouse.

Said with a smile, "Dad, can you iron this shirt" (Knows not to ask Mom)

Or "What I need is a new computer with a CD-ROM."

Out on the lawn there arose such a clatter,

The dogs spring to the fence to see what's the matter.

It's 21-year-old Derek, who's just opened a store,

"Gruven Threads" with clothes, skateboards and more.

When suddenly the phone rings from off the wall,

Justin, from U.T. giving us a call.

He's adjusting this second year, doing well in Psych at school,

Sports-oriented, working hard and naturally, being "cool."

Vance, our high school senior, will be leaving the nest.

Is this when parents finally get a rest?

It seems our motto is Dash Away, Dash Away, Dash Away All

Caught in the rush of Vance also leaving for U.T. next Fall.

Since our nest is starting to empty, it made me think of a Christmas tradition. In years prior, when the boys were younger, we would gather the toys that the boys didn't play with anymore (and toys from generous neighbors) to take the toys to the nearby Cambodian refugee families that lived near our church.

On our way, we would go to a Cambodian grocery store to buy rice and specifically Cambodian food rather than our family's grocery type food. It was a culture shock to my sons to see the raw food considered a delicacy. The presentation of raw chickens, fish and unique spices in the store were strange to them. Furthermore, it was quite a culture shock to my sons to go to a home where there was no heat on a cold winter day. Several Cambodian families were crowded into one home that was exceptionally clean but with little furniture, beds, or heat. My sons placed the bags of clothes, food and toys on the floor and tried to hide their genuine surprise at the lack of furniture and toys in the house. It simply had not been a reality to them to not own a single toy. English was not often spoken on those visits, but polite bows and smiles communicated in the most elementary way. Now it was ten years later. A beautiful Cambodian girl who had been an active church teen and now a pre-med college student revealed to me that she was a member of one of the families that we had brought toys to. The contrast of her state then as a newly arrived- refugee and the confident young lady standing before me was remarkable. She told me that she had not forgotten those Christmases or our deliveries. Of course, Justin jokes that some

Cambodian is getting wealthy today on Amazon by selling the collectible Star Wars toys that we gave away. I know he is not serious. It was a learning experience for my sons to deliver their toys to others who had none. It resulted in a personal and thought-provoking experience.

I have another favorite Christmas memory etched in my brain. Carefully, the small boy unwraps the figure from the rustling tissue paper. His hand, still dimpled from baby days, gleefully clutches the figure. "It's a shepherd," he gloats. Impatiently, his slightly older brother, with stronger fingers slides a grandmother-painted wise man from the tissue wrapper. "Oh, look—a wise man." The third and eldest boy, less impatient and with a little wonder in his voice says, "I have a wise man, too."

Slowly and amazingly gingerly, the characters of the manger scene are unwrapped. A donkey, a cow, a shepherd boy. The anticipation builds. Now a watchful, tall Joseph slides forth. Then Mary whose face reflects the peace she must have felt. Finally. . .Lo, He comes! With boyish grunts of approval from my three sons, the tiny Baby Jesus emerges from unwrapping the tissue of the grandmother-made manger box. Pleased satisfaction spreads throughout the faces of the three boys. Arranging and rearranging, they have set the scene of the manger all by themselves.

How God, too, must smile down upon us as we set the scene in our Christmas preparations. But He sees more than the outward arranging and rearranging we do. He investigates our hearts.

And from Eileen:

We thought 1996 would be a year of big changes in our lives. Some changes came off as planned; others didn't. Brett transferred from SMSU to UCONN in January. He· got a job as a news reader in the campus radio station and received a Broadcasting award at the end of the term. He also made Buchheit history by being selected to join the Golden Key National Honor Society! In true Army brat fashion, he made a place for himself in record time and is truly enjoying the campus. One of his professors, Sam Pickering, was the model for the teacher in "Dead Poet's Society." Brett told us that the quality of the courses is superior to anything he has ever experienced, as are the teachers. He made the Dean's List in Spring term and has declared Journalism as·his major -- great choice since writing and having opinions are two of his strong points! Quite a contrast to his earlier years.

Shortly after our Christmas letter last year, Brigid called off her engagement. The trip to the future in laws in Turkey was not stellar. She's working harder than ever at Young·& Rubicam, and she's moved from NJ to NYC, making her a real city slicker! Her acting bug bit again and she spent the weekends this summer at the Renaissance Fair in Tuxedo, NY as part of the improv players. She had such a good time that she's going back for their next extravaganza and looking for other opportunities in theatre-rich NYC!

Eileen continues teaching at TPU. Her evaluation from a student was, "...super good, but very strong." That translates into, "...actually expects students to work." Oh, well. The main campus in Tokyo sent a rep to observe in CT. He then issued an invitation to come to Japan to work for 4 weeks on methods and content. Since there's no firm date, the bags have yet to be packed. In her spare time, she and a friend are incorporating and developing games devoted to students studying English as a Foreign Language.

Joe has his 4th job at Sikorsky in as many years. He now manages an international team of marketers, proposals and depot experts. Those people have taken some of the travel burden from Joe, but he doesn't seem to get home any earlier. Guess expanding the farm may take some more years. We were visited by our good friend,

Jim Ducharme, this August, and the formerly derelict greenhouse is now rebuilt thanks to Jim. Of course, Jim is a bit of a perfectionist, so we've renamed the structure "The Gold House," as we replaced all the wood with pressure treated timbers and most of the 64 panes of glass, few of which were anything but standard$$$!

On a sad note, our infamous dog, Harry, was hit by a car last spring and died, He was our staunch protector and resident nut case for 15 years, sometimes keeping the neighbors and us in stitches -- other times, panic. In a moment of madness, we went to the pound and adopted a puppy. He turns out to be a Newfoundland, a species that grows to be the size of a small city. His name is "Roo", so called by Nana because he jumps like a kangaroo. The adventure continues! Louie is not too sure of our sanity-- we, on the other hand, have no doubts?!

"This Old House" will be in transition for many years to come!

Let's Discuss:

1) How does Christmas make you feel: happy, sad, excited, lonely, etc.? How do you focus yourself and/or your family on the true meaning of Christmas and the Good News?

2) The Wise Men traveled to see the child Jesus after he was born. Instead of seeking gifts from Jesus, they greeted him with joy and gifts. What gifts do you give Jesus?

3) With what gifts has God blessed you?

4) Have you thought about the sacrifices some people have made to give you a gift? Are there gifts that you have received in the past that you didn't fully appreciate at that time?

5) One of God's greatest gifts to the people of Israel in the past had been freedom. As we prepare for Christmas, should we look at the ways we are not free. Perhaps we are a captive of our past on a treadmill to prove something to ourselves or others? Is there a gift of freedom we should give to ourselves

Visit to Fairview Farm; Brenda, David, Eileen

V

Christmas Countdown, 1997

From Brenda: I have good news and bad news. After we returned from a mission trip for Dave and Sue Long's Bermuda church, David went to the doctor. He had unusual exhaustion and bruising. The diagnosis was Acute Lymphocytic Leukemia. Good friends John and Christy Fonvielle volunteered to drive us to Houston to enter M.D. Anderson. The good news is that M.D. Anderson is admitting us, and some of the chemo treatment can be back in Fort Worth. David and I see this as a faith journey. The irony is that his intensive chemotherapy is beginning as Vance is starting as a Freshman at U.T. and our nest was emptying. Justin is now a junior at U.T.

David has always been the wind beneath my wings. I think now we must fall into formation with God as lead goose and let God's jet stream sustain us for this difficult but do-able journey. We just hope we don't quack up. . .I'm so glad God has a sense of humor. We're trying!

Now that it is Christmas, David has finished his 5th round of chemotherapy. He has kept his weight but lost his hair. We have a new understanding of bald is beautiful which is good news.

Other good news. Derek has gotten engaged to Melody McLain who is from Colorado Springs. They will be getting married March 21,1998 during Spring Break in picturesque Woodland Park, Colorado. Derek, being a budding entrepreneur, has enjoyed his clothes store of "Gruven Threads" but the monthly bills outweighed his grooving customers. He closed the store but is going to pursue his multiple entrepreneurial ideas.

Justin pledged a business fraternity and quarterbacked their intramural football team. He told us they were doing well. It turned out his team not only made it to the Playoffs but won! They became Intramural Champions defeating the Legal Eagles (Law School team). He said it probably will be the only time he outmaneuvers an attorney. John Grisham look out! So, Justin's name is on the Honor Wall of intramurals in Gregory Gym at U.T. At the same time, David's name from the late 1960's is on the same wall, as his intramural team (Tejas Club) was a co-champion while he quarterbacked. An interesting circle of life.

Vance has made it through his Freshman Fall semester. He pledged Fiji (Phi Gamma Delta), so his plans for Christmas are sleeping and eating just in time to rush out the door to visit old friends.

Speaking of friends, so many times we have found that light, a point of reference, to be the people of God. They have been light bearers for us, creating a haven in some dark moments. For example, Christy and John taking us to Houston. The difference has helped us to rely on a God of comfort, strength, and love in this chemotherapy journey.

Meanwhile, Eileen was recovering from a strange onset of illness. This is what we hear from Eileen:
A belated but very merry Christmas!

As some of you know, my husband gave me an amazing birthday gift this year- a return trip to England! The purpose of the trip- other than fun! - was to trace our Irish ancestors who stayed in England prior to immigrating to America. Liverpool was their final location before sailing. In the case of the Ayers family, we have their address in Liverpool, as well as the names of two churches where their first two children were baptized.

Unfortunately, I found that traveling from the church locations to their address was like going from Freeport, Long Island to Westchester- with no car! I also learned- from a helpful policeman- that their final address was in a "bad part of the docks" and probably was as bad - or worse- when the Ayers clan bid farewell to Liverpool. A good place to be FROM. Lastly, I learned that if you're going to be violently ill, this is not the place to be. I ended up spending a week in my hotel room with doctors for room service. The score is Ghosts 7- Eileen 1. I'll be back!

Let's Talk!

It is nothing like an illness to get our attention. From bald is beautiful to being sick far away from home stops us in our tracks. It is only when we lose the good health that we take for granted, that we understand what a gift that good health is!

Ecclesiastes 5:19 (NIV) "Moreover, when God gives someone wealth and possessions, and the ability of good health to enjoy them, to accept their lot and be happy in their work—this is a gift of God."

1) Have you ever been sick at Christmas so that you can't do it all? Have you begun to see that others may be strong where you are weak, and you do not have to be all things to all people?

2) Have you given thought to someone who is sick at Christmas and how you might make their Christmas cheerier? Or personally delivered help to a deserving family?

   When David was enduring chemotherapy in numerous week-long hospital trips to M.D. Anderson in Houston, a neighbor and friend dropped off a poinsettia plant on my doorstep. The handwritten note said, "Thinking of you." It is hard to put into words the cheer that the little flowering plant brought me as I faced the Christmas ahead. I have never forgotten that moment as I bent over to pick up the plant left on my doorstep. Even though I have had other kindnesses, at that very moment, a little poinsettia plant and thoughtfulness was what I needed.

3) What have been the darkest seasons of your life? How did you make it through those seasons?

4) Sometimes good comes from something broken. It was Christmas Eve in 1818 in a tiny village in the Austrian Alps called Oberndorf. The pipe organ had broken, and the assistant pastor was wondering what they would do for the

Midnight Mass. He remembered a poem he had written at his previous parish. So, he took it to the parish organist and asked if he could create a simple tune that could be played on the guitar. The priest's verses were not great, just true words and in that tiny village some 200 years ago, "Silent Night" was first sung. In the years that followed, the song began to travel by word of mouth slowly as folk songs do. And from that broken organ, one of the most cherished Christmas songs was written. Has something good come from your brokenness?

Christmas Countdown, 1998

From Brenda: Radiating health with a shiny dome and firm handshake is David—hair today and gone tomorrow. It's been a hair-raising journey this year. We have learned a lot and the Christmas season helps bring our last year's journey into focus. The three Magi traveled from the East to pay homage to the infant Jesus. They brought three gifts: gold, frankincense, and myrrh.

Gold is a precious metal used for money and wealth. We have had a wealth of support with prayers, food, baskets of cards and loving friends who have called, inquired, cared and prayed.

The second gift of **frankincense** was a very fragrant gum resin used in incense. David and I both have learned that every day is a gift—that's why it's called the present. This makes you appreciate your senses—enjoying the fresh smell of sunshine and new grass at a father/son (Vance) golf tournament at U.T. on a windy, clear day in May. Going fly fishing in the summer in Colorado with Justin & Vance, stepping into a cold sparkling river, contrasted with the warmth of the sun beating on your back as you stroke the line or feel the unexpected delight of a quick mountain rain brushing your face. How about basking in a warm Texas backyard hammock and staring up the lattice of pecan tree leaves and sunlight above your head. David says feeling the contrast of peppy energy returning and building back slowly from the hard zap of chemo is slow and welcome. David also says feeling the wind in your new grown buzz from chemotherapy is a thrill.

The third gift was **myrrh**, a fragrant gum resin used in perfume. That, too, is a sweetness and joy of the senses. From the gentle fragrance of mountain flowers at our eldest son Derek's Spring wedding and the unending smiles and blushes of the bride and groom, to the joy that Melody and Derek have now announced at Christmas that next Spring will bring our first grandchild. Lo and behold, the sonogram says it is a girl. There is joy in that Derek has all the signs of a proud and responsible father. There is further joy in going to the Fall Parent's Weekend at UT and seeing the two fine young men that Justin and Vance have become. Truly David and I both feel the joy at the gift of remission since David gained remission without having to undergo a bone marrow transplant. He has continued to maintain his job and keep a strong work schedule despite the chemo regimen for this year. The regimen is one week of chemo at the hospital and three weeks off to work and regain stamina.

Wise men that the Magi were, they recognized the precious nature of their gifts and they lay them at the foot of the manger. They gave gifts. We would do the same.

Let's hear from Eileen who had a topsy turvy year as only total renovation can bring.

As I sit here writing this, I'm taking a mental inventory of all that's happened in the last year. It all began so innocently...

We neared completion of our kitchen renovation in January. {Joe's translation, "We're closer to 'done' than on day one.") We {Joe's translation, "We??!!") decided to do some mini projects in the living room. {Joe's translation, "Mini as in building the pyramids.") After removing the barn board, lathe and plaster from the fireplace wall, those dangerous words "We might as well" were first uttered. It took on its own life force. 'We might as well put in electrified sconces, insulation, outlets, new wall board, millwork around the fireplace, rip out the windows..." At some point, we (Joe's translation, "There's that 'we' again!!") decided to put in a tin ceiling, too.

Suddenly, it was spring. As you know, in the spring, a middle-aged woman's fancy lightly turns to thoughts of re-finishing flooring. {Joe's translation, "A middle-aged man's fancy turns to hernias.") With the help of Brigid's boyfriend, Tim, out came three or four layers of kitchen flooring.

Suddenly, it was Fall. Awaiting the delivery of the new kitchen floor, we found ourselves without water. Digging a well was a new experience, a tad on the expensive side. (Joe's translation, "Pick a vein-I'm bled out!) We now have a 650-foot well and- please God- enough water for a small city.

Suddenly, it was Christmas. OK, so the floor's not in and the tin ceiling is up but not finished (Joe's translation, "Ever count the number of nails you need to touch up on a tin ceiling?!") The millwork is almost done- no translation, Joe!! The important thing is that we're all fine, or as close as we can be under the circumstances, looking forward to Santa's visit. {Joe's translation, "Have him drink some well water!") and wishing you every joy at Christmas and all year through.

Let's Talk:

1) When in your life has some Christmas project gone differently than you expected? What happened?

2) The wise men brought presents to Jesus to honor him. Do you see how these gifts met his future financial needs (escape to Egypt) and fit in God's plans? Can you name some of the ways the gifts honored him?

3) What unintended meanings have you found in your Christmas celebrations? (For example, we give gifts because the wise men brought gifts) In what ways could these gifts or celebrations be God talking to you personally?

4) When children set up a manger scene, they often crowd the wise men and shepherds around the baby Jesus, so Jesus becomes completely hidden by the crowd around him. And yet, this is God's arrangement that Jesus becomes wonderful and personal to each person coming to worship even in crowded situations. Has He personalized your Christmas this year? Have you sought Him in the crowds? Do you have a manger scene that you can thoughtfully and slowly unwrap to imagine what each one was thinking the night of Jesus birth?

Christmas Countdown, 1999

Once again, we take stock of the last year's "events". This year's highs and lows have been higher and lower than usual. Let's start with Eileen.

Among the highs for Brett were graduation from U.Conn. with a degree in journalism, which he used to get his first job as a reporter for the New Milford Times. It was good experience for him, and he continues to send in stories from his new location-Africa! He entered the Peace Corps last summer, flying to Rabat, Morocco to begin his Arabic studies. By September, he completed his courses and was assigned to Tetouan where he works on an erosion control project. Joe arrived there in time for the swearing in ceremony at the Ambassador's residence-for a while there it looked like Joe had signed on, too!

Brigid left Elizabeth Arden to join Avon's international division. She shuttles back and forth from their offices in NYC to Rye, NY where their think tank is located. Her background in advertising, cosmetics and foreign languages made this a perfect match. Last month she moved into a brownstone apartment in Manhattan. She worked the Renaissance Faire in Tuxedo, NY last summer and will be in their ads for next season- watch for our poster child!

Joe made a major change as well, leaving Sikorsky for Kaman Aerospace-- a manufacturer of naval helicopters. Kaman recently made some major sales in Egypt, Australia and New Zealand and decided to expand its ILS Department. He is the new Vice President, Customer Support.

This is a longer commute, but he's enjoying the ride in his new car.
Eileen will be leaving her job at Naugatuck Valley this semester. She's decided that working for a psycho is hazardous to her health and would prefer working on a textbook she's been writing off and on. This also makes it possible to travel with Joe - Morocco anyone?! Under "other duties" we include the additions to the farm menagerie- 2 full size donkeys, originally 6- now 5- (don't ask!) guinea hens and 2 black sheep, creatively named "Baa-Baa" and "Black Sheep"!

Our sad news comes in reporting the passing of Eileen's mother, "Nana Nurse", last July. She died after a long illness and a month in ICU. Three surgeries in a year's time were too much even for her remarkable recuperative powers. She is sorely missed.

From Brenda: Well, I have been busy learning!

A man found a cocoon of a butterfly. One day a small opening appeared. He sat and watched the butterfly for several hours as it struggled to force its body through that little hole.

Then it seemed to stop making any progress. It appeared as if it had gotten as far as it could, and it could go no further.

The man decided to help the butterfly. He took a pair of scissors and snipped off the remaining bit of the cocoon. The butterfly then emerged easily. But it had a swollen body and small, shriveled wings.

The man continued to watch the butterfly because he expected that, at any moment, the wings would enlarge and expand to be able to support the body, which would contract in time.

Neither happened! In fact, the butterfly spent the rest of its short life crawling around with a swollen body and shriveled wings. It was never able to fly.

What the man, in his kindness and haste, did not understand was that the restricting cocoon and the struggle required for the butterfly to get through the tiny opening were God's way of forcing fluid from the body of the butterfly into its wings so that it would be ready for flight once it achieved its freedom from the cocoon.

Sometimes struggles are exactly what we need in our lives. If God allowed us to go through our lives without any obstacles, it would cripple us. We would not be as strong as what we could have been. We could never fly!

This is what I read recently and perhaps it will be exactly what you need to read, too

—I asked for Strength. And God gave me Difficulties to make me strong.

I asked for wisdom. And God gave me problems to solve.

I asked for love. And God gave me troubled people to help.

I asked for favors. And God gave me opportunities.

I received nothing I wanted. I received everything I needed!

So, it seems that the Lord is continuing with us on our cancer journey and is giving everything, we need. This Christmas, like the rest of the world, we are looking forward to the new century and the year 2000. For us, 2000 brings the hope of a cure for the leukemia with a now needed bone marrow transplant. Due to a mild heart attack in June, David's chemo had to be stopped. David has come out of remission. This leaves only a transplant option. None of David's sons or brothers was a bone marrow match. However, we found a bone marrow match from a kind stranger in Minnesota. We do not know his name. We are thanking God for the kindness of strangers!! In late January, David will go to M.D. Anderson to begin the long process of a bone marrow transplant which will give a permanent cure.

1999 also brought us the joy of our first grandchild. Derek and Melody gave birth to a beautiful baby girl named Skylar Eden Shull in January. We arrived at the hospital in the early A.M. to see the proud parents. Derek decided to let his swaddled child sleep on his chest. He stretched out on the comfy couch near Melody's bed. Unfortunately, the new dad was exhausted. He awoke shortly afterward in a panic. Skylar was no longer on his chest! Fearing the worst—had he squashed his new daughter? Had she rolled onto the floor? Wildly he checked beneath the couch and in the cushion. The nurse walked in the room. Fortunately, she had taken the baby back to the nursery but had mercifully left the new dad to get some sleep. Also, fortunately, she had not told the exhausted new mom about this scenario. As a proud new grandfather, David has already begun the pleasure of reading to his grandchild just as he did when the boys were little.

June brought Justin's graduation from the University of Texas at Austin. Both David and I, our other two sons and my parents witnessed this achievement ceremony. Justin plans to work in Austin. He plans on pursuing an MBA in the future. Vance is continuing his undergraduate studies at U.T.

David and I celebrated our 32nd wedding anniversary in June. He had a business trip to Alaska, so we combined business with pleasure and flew to the Kenai peninsula. He was weakened so I did all the driving, but it was a good trip to be on an adventure together once again. The last time he had a business trip to Alaska was twenty years before when Vance was a newborn. It made our anniversary special to celebrate in Alaska and poignant, too! It is a role reversal for me because David has always been the strong one. We are thankful for the opportunities of 2000 and the milestone achievements of 1999!

Let's Talk

1) In what areas of your life are you anxious for quick resolution like emerging from a cocoon? How can you better gain strength and courage while waiting?

2) Think of something you wanted and later received, for which you had to wait. Now think of something you wanted and received immediately. Which was more meaningful in the end?

3) We cannot see the wind, but we can feel it. It is the same way with God's Spirit. The Holy Spirit cannot be seen,

but he can be felt in our lives. Have you trusted that he would guide us in every step of our walk with Jesus?

4) We've all heard that "patience is a virtue," but we're anxious for fast results in our lives. Just like children we want fast food and quick opening of presents on Christmas morning. Psalm 27:14 says, "Wait for the Lord; be strong, and let your heart take courage; wait for the Lord!" Has God called you to wait for answers?

Christmas Countdown, 2000

First, let's hear from Eileen about her family's millennium experience:

> *As usual, we've been on life's roller coaster and have had more than the expected number of ups and downs. Here's this year's saga!*
>
> *Brett returned from the Peace Corps and set out to bike across America to raise money for cancer research. Unfortunately, the folks who said they'd go along dropped out, so he went solo – 2 months and 3031 miles later – Bridgeport, CT to San Diego, CA.! After he caught his breath – and his mother started breathing again – he left for Washington, DC. He found a fundraising job in the largest private orphanage in the USA and plans to stay there until he starts Law School next fall. Amazing!*

Brigid fulfilled a life-long dream in the spring when she adopted "La Dolce Vida", a Palomino Quarter Horse. "Vida" is a beauty -looks like "Trigger" for those old enough to remember Roy Rogers! Unfortunately, Brigid had a serious riding accident during the summer, breaking and dislocating her ankle. That caused her to be laid up through fall. She made good use of her time and wrote a book! Who knows – she may be the American Agatha Christie?! Her second surgery was completed in November, and she is in physical therapy again until the new year. Her millennium has brought physical challenges unexpected for one so young.

Joe keeps those frequent flyer miles pumping for Kaman. His latest trips have been to Egypt, Australia, and New Zealand. Eileen made two trips to Egypt this year: if you hear "See the pyramids along the Nile..." playing in the background, you know what we felt!

Eileen's textbook proposal is with the publishers now and she's back in the classroom again. The Regional Schools needed someone to take over their ESL department. It's part time and there's still the chance to hop on a plane with Joe- a perfect combination!

Our "farm" continues to grow- a glorified petting zoo! Come and see us for the new millennium (BRING CARROTS!!!)

While we had ups and downs the downs were temporary. The same was not true for Brenda. We lost a good friend in David with his death in April due to complications of pneumonia from the bone marrow transplant. It was an almost three-year fight. Brenda lost a 33-year lover, husband, and friend.

From Brenda:
This year has brought a blur of past, present, and future—a year where memories have collided with present realities daily.

First, picture the Thanksgiving table in our first Thanksgiving without David. All of us are surrounding the table for a photograph. What you don't know is that the turkey is still basking in the oven and is an hour late. You see, David always took care of the turkey and I'm still getting the hang of the timing of it. However, since it was late, everyone was starved and thought it was delicious. I keep finding that gratitude can turn a negative into a positive.

You can see Vance. He is in the Business School at U.T. and is on the predictable 5-year plan (which means not this year but next year graduation). He calls the Fifth year a Victory Lap. He's interning at Merrill Lynch.

Meanwhile Justin is working at Janus Mutual Fund in Austin. I have noticed that once these guys get to Austin, they don't seem to want to leave Austin.

Next to him is Melody, Derek and Skylar who now live in Denver. Skylar has just ripped off a wonderful bow in her baby blond hair. The bow was Gram's idea. Skylar will be two in January and from an unbiased viewpoint is exceptionally beautiful, smart and verbally advanced. Her mom called to Skylar when Skylar and Gram (that's me) were playing in a back bedroom. She lifted her head up to answer her mom's call and her little face became perplexed. She knew to run to her mom, but she and Gram were having a lot of fun playing. So, mustering up her courage, she shook herself as she answered back, "I **busy**!" To hear an 18-month-old toddler decide not to run to mommy where she feared the consequences but felt she had to take a stand, was funny. It was a mirror of an adult answer. And so goes life.

Nelson Mandela said, "May your choices reflect your hopes, not your fears." And so, you wonder, what am I doing and how am I coping since David's death in April? Losing a partner, lover and friend left a huge hole that is bigger and deeper than I even imagined. I have a pain in my back, opposite where my heart is. For his funeral, we lined up to proceed as a family down the aisle. Subconsciously, I reached aside for his hand, looking around momentarily for him, confused that he wasn't by my side. Where could he be? He had always been there for almost 33 years. Then it all rushed back to me, and I remembered.

I told a friend that what I really want to do is to run down the street screaming but I have restrained myself. I bounce off the walls which are surprisingly padded with tender mercies. Daily some kindness has come my way to make it easier. When I woke up the morning after he died, out of the air these words came to me, "Morning by morning new mercies I see." Yes, those are the words from a hymn that came to me unbidden. These tender mercies have ranged from the doctor who came in on his day off to be present when we had to take David off the ventilator, to the woman from Saudi Arabia who wanted to sing "Ave Maria" for us before we left the hospital the last time, to my friend Ann in Denver and Eileen in Connecticut whose homes I escaped for respite, to Jan who arranged food and Sandra and Suzann who helped plan an escape trip to the North East around my birthday. To a Christmas poinsettia left on my doorstep since this is our first Christmas without him, to an annual delivered smoked turkey for Christmas from the Craddocks, to the Smarts who donated flight miles so I could fly back and forth to Houston during David's transplant, to neighbors who anonymously mow the lawn, to friends who pop an encouraging card or email my way or take me to lunch. The list amazes me with thoughtful tender mercies both large and small. I know God is behind it all.

David accomplished more in his short 55 years than many who live to a ripe old age. To honor David in perpetuity, not one but three scholarship funds have been set up by friends: at U.T. Austin for the Tejas Club where he was a member, to Paschal High School (to be given to a senior boy and girl) where he was a dad and Booster Club officer and at Broadway Baptist for the youth choir group to attend the global choir trips. David modeled and taught us how to die with courage and a selflessness that is hard to comprehend.

What else have I learned?

- It is the difficult times during which you grow, whether you want to or not. Just like the caterpillar to butterfly process, it is not to be cut short if you are truly going to fly.
- I am more aware of my limitations which gives me the opportunity for my improvement, to depend on God and gives others the chance to pick up my slack. I am not a superhero. I need people.
- Life is what taps you on the shoulder when you are busy planning something else. But God remains in control when everything else seems out of control.
- Women are like tea bags. Put them in hot water and they get stronger.
- David was the wind beneath my wings. Now, without treasured friends, I would forget how to fly.

Let's Talk!

1) Have you experienced profound loss? Can you think of others who need your tender mercy this Christmas season? How can you reach out not only to the less fortunate but also to those who might be hurting?

2) How do you cope with profound loss or a life changing experience?

3) Have you or those you know turned away from God because of great pain? In Romans 11:36 Paul knew the reality of great, unexplainable sorrow but he came to realize that God is humanity's only real hope. As Paul considered God's great mercies, he was lost in wonder, love and praise.

4) Christmas begins when we take the time to show love through simple acts. Are we mourning Christmas past or comforted by the joy of Christmas present? Can you think of ways to give to others that will in turn help you through Christmas?

Christmas Countdown, 2001

From Brenda: It is the year of 9/11. Just like the rest of the world, we at the Shull house are trying to adjust to a new normal. For many in the United States, it was a new normal following the terrorist attack on the twin towers in New York City. This is the first year of George W. Bush's term. The White House did not allow tourists for the Christmas White House tour to honor those who died but also it was necessary for safety purposes. We can't help but look backward at our year with some sadness, but we do look forward with joy. Because of 9/11, this was a very important time to think about what is important in your life and to never miss the opportunity to admit to someone you love them. We never know when we leave someone's presence, if that is the last time, we will see them on this earth. We all have the responsibility to embrace each day as if it is a gift.

As we look back in sadness, we still try to adjust to a world without David. This year, when it had been one year since David's death, my mother had a life-ending cerebral hemorrhage. She was tending my dad who had unexpected critical surgery. He was recuperating in intensive care, and she was in his room. Without warning she had an intensive headache and suffered a massive and eventual fatal stroke at the age of 76, one year after David's death. For three weeks I was rotating between two critical care units for my dad and for my mom. The sound and smell of a hospital room sent me into headaches daily. My dad recuperated from his bout in time to bury his sweetheart of 57 years. He is trying to adjust to a new normal.

Christmas was my mother's favorite time of year. She always started decorating in October in every corner of the house. Not only did she dye the sandwich bread red and green, but she even had her poodles dyed red and green when they were groomed. As I said, she was frenetic about Christmas doings. We all remember her spiked Christmas punch that she dipped into several times. Through it all, she had an unwavering faith in God and love of Christmas.

As we adjust to the impact of 2001, we can only look forward. We know that 2002 brings joy: We happily plan for Vance to graduate next May from the Business School at U.T. Justin has decided to begin his MBA at SMU next Fall so he will be moving back to Dallas. The best news of all is that I'm gaining another daughter. Ashley Craddock will join our family on June 22, 2002, when she and Vance are married in Dallas. In the meantime, Derek and Melody continue to thrive in Colorado with the laughter and the wonder of their daughter Skylar who somehow has avoided the terrible twos with her sweetness and light.

So, we greet Christmas time with the knowledge that each day is a gift—that is why it is called the present. May you and your family enjoy the gift of the present and the gift of God's love in these holy days.

Happy Holidays from Eileen! In taking stock of our comings and goings for 2001, there's proof that you can never tell what will happen next in life. After more than 30 years in aviation, Joe has changed direction. He stayed in supply chain management but in a new industry. He is the new VP of Procurement/Vendor Management, United Health Group and has spent the year showing how to apply manufacturing techniques to the health care industry. Tall order! The good news is that he loves the challenge – and that, in changing jobs, we managed not to change house. (It would have been 31 moves in 31 years of marriage!). We really do love it here in Bridgewater and Joe finds the commute doable!

Eileen is still having fun and getting paid for it – nice combination. As her ESL students graduate, no new ones enroll, so there could be a retirement in her future just 3 short years from now - a devastating blow to Joe! Last summer brought a new pottery kiln into her life and she is re-discovering an old love for things ceramic (Maybe her new direction?!). She's holding out for a potting wheel next - we'll have to see what Santa brings, little girl.........

Brigid changed jobs in November and is enjoying her new role as Marketing Coordinator in Hartford also at United Health Group. She commutes with her dad daily – lots of bonding time – do you see a dynasty in the making?

Brett loves his job in DC and hopes to go to law school next fall. After filling out countless applications, it's in God's hands – but feel free to add your own prayers!

Once again, we have adds and losses in the animal kingdom. Two new lambs (Beauty and Big Ass) came at Easter Time- never mention "spring lamb" to them – it makes them nervous! Our geriatric adoptees keep popping off on a regular basis and Steven King's Pet Cemetery is alive and well (?!) in our back pasture. Since the animal control office hasn't sent us any nasty grams recently, guess we're in the clear for another year. Boomer and Roo still rule the roost. Jenny, the donkey, continues to keep the coyotes at bay.

Along with new roofs for the barn and house, we've added a pond and waterfall to our back garden along with an expanded stone patio on both sides of the pool. "Better Homes and Gardens" keeps calling to do a feature story but we are keeping a low profile! (Do you believe that? Not so much). At this rate, there will be nothing familiar about our 160+ year old house by the time retirement comes.

Let's Talk:

In both Eileen and Brenda's life, change was unexpected and brought a new normal.

1) What has the new normal been in your life and how has it affected your Christmas celebration?
   Look at Isaiah 49:11 And I will make all my mountains a road, and my highways shall be raised up.
   Does that sound like we should take the high road? How have you taken the high road?

2) Because of 9/11, this was a very important time to think about what is important in your life and to never miss the opportunity to admit to someone you love them.
   Have you taken the time to say the words that you know are true and that someone needs to hear you say-- "I love you"? Sometimes knowing is not enough. Hearing the words is more important.

3) How did 9/11 affect you? Were you alive and do you remember how you felt? Did it affect your understanding of a new normal?

4) God's purposes at the end are exactly what they were at the beginning. God does not change, so His promises and plans do not change. Every believer receives the tremendous blessing of a changed heart with new power to obey. Have you personally experienced that God's mercy is inclusive, not exclusive? Have you asked God to be included in his mercy with a personal experience? If not, isn't it time?

Christmas Countdown, 2002

From Brenda:

Happiness and pain. We welcome the one and fear the other, yet they are intertwined through our lives. They are the conduits that lead us to God, who created us to dance. . .to weep... to love life.. .and to feed his sheep. We are a society that craves feeling good. As we mature, we discover eventually that we truly do make our own happiness. We are as happy as we will allow ourselves to be. Pure joy comes most often when we are at peace with ourselves and obey. "Be still and know that I am God." (Psalm 46:10). Being still is something I haven't quite mastered.

Joy is often tinged with sadness. Joy is a mountain top experience. Reaching the top is a great view, but it also means there is a downside to it. When we feel great joy, it is usually the result of an aspiration that has come true. It is accompanied by change. Even the joyful birth of a child means giving up the life you had before.

Melody and Derek continue happily living in Denver with their thriving three-year-old. A child brings daily changes.

Ashley and Vance have experienced change, following a glorious and picture-perfect wedding at Highland Park Presbyterian. The bride, the wedding, the reception was beautiful. They are happily adjusting to the changes brought by marriage. They are thriving with life in the fast lane in Dallas while she teaches, and Vance pursues real estate development.

Achieving an educational milestone or an important job promotion means both happiness and bittersweet pain. The thrill of the pursuit is over and there is some adrenaline loss. Sometimes there are even battle scars from trying to push to our accomplishments, but these are present in a life well lived. These are evidence that we dared to love, hope, and dream as we step outside our comfort zone. Justin is experiencing the stress of long hours in graduate school. There is nothing like graduate school to scar or intimidate a student's ego. Justin believes that graduate students inflate a professor's ego. He remarked that if ego were a country, his professor's would be China. Hmm. I assume he thinks that graduate professor is a little arrogant.

And yes, this year has brought a major change in my life. I have decided to find happiness and grab the golden ring. Or, in this case, a diamond ring. Following a year- long courtship, I have married. This meant I had to sell my twenty-year home in Fort Worth. It was bittersweet as I closed that chapter. But we have purchased a lovely home in Colleyville with fountains and lake view for a happily ever after home. I have dared to dance. . .and embrace life.

Speaking of the happiness and pain from change, we hear from Eileen:

Once again, we are in career transition – so, what's new? After almost 3 years of a killer commute, Joe has left Kaman and is looking for greener, closer pastures. He's still trying to decide what he wants to do when he grows up....

Brigid has spent the last year with Cendant Mobility. It's a huge relocation corporation that owns everything from the moving vans to the real estate company. She's working on- get this- Military relocations!! She certainly is experienced in that arena!

Brett is still in Washington, DC. He's clerking in a law firm. It looks like there will be another lawyer in the family. That's what comes of watching too much "LA Law" in your formative years. The good news is that he's getting some amazing experience and has found he has a real aptitude and appetite for this legal stuff- go figure!

Eileen is still enjoying her job with region 12 schools. Now that she knows the staff and the system, she's finding ways to fund students' activities like bowling, movies, dance and art classes, justifying all this as part of the American experience. – she's good at finding the back door into the finance department!

The farm still brings us joy and is a constant source of entertainment- and some disappointments. This year we had a tough lesson in farming; Joe learned that there are area plants that should not be fed to the animals, such as mountain laurel and rhododendron. We lost all the sheep, with half the goat population being sick for months. Someone alluded to Joe's penchant for reading Steven King and another friend mentioned "Pet Cemetery" as the new name for our Fair View Farm.

We also lost Louie, our Chesapeake Bay retriever, this year to crippling arthritis after only 9 years with us. We'll miss him a great deal. Joe thought we'd be a one dog family again until Eileen came home with a pedigree Black Lab she was introduced to at the vets! Shades of Harry, this one, aptly named Boomer, has 2 screws loose....

Anyhow, we've had another full year and are ready to dance.

Let's Talk:

As Brenda said, Joy is often tinged with sadness. Joy is a mountain top experience. Reaching the top is a great view, but it also means there is a downside to it. Even the joyful birth of a child means giving up the life you had before. Or remarrying and merging into a new blended family.

1) What mountaintop experiences have you had this year? Has it been a roller coaster? Have you tried for a joyful time alone with the Lord to get to know Him especially in this Christmas season?
   Jonah 2:6 At the roots of the mountains, I went down to the land whose bars closed upon me forever; yet you brought up my life from the pit, O Lord my God.

2) Or Isaiah 52:7 How beautiful upon the mountains are the feet of him who brings good news, who publishes peace, who brings good news of happiness, who publishes salvation, who says to Zion, "Your God reigns." Have you noticed lately how your God reigns? What does this look life in your life?

3) How has your understanding of the Christmas story evolved as you experienced life's journey? When were you at the pits and when were you at the heights? What helped you?

4) God can use change to bring about a deeper faith and understanding of His will for us. What does Ecclesiastes 3:1 mean to you? "There is a time for everything and a season for every activity under the heavens."

Christmas Countdown, 2003

From Brenda:

It was the racing toward Christmas—rushed rituals, drive-through dinners, both spouses working, Martha expectations that brought me to—silence. I realized once again that silence is the language of God. It is not a roar, but a whisper. For in silence, we tend to focus on the important and the priorities of the heart. In silence we prepare for mysteries that may lie ahead.

Melody and Derek have decided to pursue Derek's dream of involvement in successful night clubs. They decided to move from Colorado to the pinnacle of nightclubs. They have moved to Las Vegas. They are adjusting to the climate change from Colorado Springs/Denver to Las Vegas. Skylar, a truly beautiful and significantly intelligent, articulate, and all-around superior child will be 5 years old in January. Sigh! says the grandmother of a single grandchild!

Ashley and Vance have celebrated one year of marriage and purchased their first home in Dallas. This means Vance has been re-introduced to lawn work. Vance had commented on how he loved the canopy of large old trees in his neighborhood-- until Fall leaves covered the lawn. Now, not so much. Ashley teaches at a private preschool and Vance has begun his first year pursuing his MBA at Texas Christian University. He is surviving a commute of an hour one way to Fort Worth. Fortunately, he says the traffic is mostly going the opposite direction from him or it would be longer. With the long hours of being a graduate assistant and student, he's looking forward to some rest at Christmas.

Also looking forward to time off is Justin. He is continuing his second year at SMU and hopes to graduate next May. He has visions of a Spring job search. But he found one of the better assignments in his graduate degree is international business. For this assignment, he chose to go to Argentina. I thought it was to use his Spanish capability. I had paid for an international language course in Spain in his undergraduate years. Then I found out that this Argentine assignment also included an Argentine hunting trip. Evidently Argentina offers the ultimate dove hunting which tops all bird hunting trips. It would appear all is not suffering and endurance as a graduate student for Justin.

The same goes for me. My husband and I are both working but sneak off with any excuse for a vacation now that we are empty nesters and newlyweds. We went to Hawaii with my sister and her husband for Spring Break, then to Alaska for our mutual birthdays, and France for our one-year anniversary. On the weekends, we attempt golf. We have barely broken 100 plus. However, creative score keeping, and toe kicks have helped our game. Tiger Woods and Anika don't appear to be worried.

From Eileen:

While 2002 was, in many ways, a year best forgotten, 2003 has been memorable in positive ways\ Here's the rundown ... alphabetically!

Brett started Law School in August- the "Paper Chase" is on! He is studying at the Appalachian School of Law in "scenic" Grundy, Virginia. He is one of about 100 students, down from 125. That's an indication of the level of stress, and of the expectations of the faculty. What was "excellent" before is just "OK" now. Still, knowing the level of determination in our Number One Son, I almost pity the person who tries to rain on his parade!

Brigid has also had an amazing year. She started off with a promotion to Manager of the Flexible Spending Program. Then, much to our delight, she became engaged to Tim Carney in October. It would be hard to list all Tim's good qualities here, so let's just say that his favorite restaurant is "Casa de Buchheit" and that he shares Joe's enthusiasm for all things tool related! They plan a fall wedding. It's yet to be decided what role their baby Great Dane, Colossus, will play – perhaps "Flower Dog"?

Eileen will see two of her favorite students graduate this spring. These girls spoke no English when they arrived five years ago. Now both are honor roll students and are deciding which college they'll attend in the fall. How can you ask for more as a teacher? In her free time (all animals sleep eventually!), Eileen has been firing loads of ceramics in her kiln. Joe supplies the long arms and muscle necessary, along with comments about the power bills!

Joe has been busy at home and at work. The projects in "This Old House" this year included installing central air conditioning and the purchase of a new tractor. He promptly entered it in the annual (YES, ANNUAL!) Bridgewater Tractor Parade and won an award in the "Single Tractor Category". (For those of you who have never experienced the Tractor Parade, keep the Sunday of the Labor Day weekend open next year!)

When the farm is not calling his name, he's still taking on the challenges at work. This year brought a symposium in Jamaica- not Queens for our New York contingent! Eileen's suitcase was packed before the ink on the tickets was dry – a week in paradise ... during hurricane season? Does anyone see a problem there?! Still, we made it home... eventually!

Let's Talk!

At this point in time, both Eileen and Brenda enjoyed weddings in the family. Although they were not at Christmas, the celebration is worth commenting on. Planning for a wedding brings story book expectations. Brenda's new daughter-in-law started a wish book when she was in middle school for her "someday" wedding. When the time came, Ashley just needed to fill in the groom's name because she had many choices already in her head. Her wedding was indeed storybook with a purple rose for each female guest, and a large wedding party of friends from childhood, camp, and college. Guests filled the sanctuary of one of Dallas's largest churches. Brenda was happy her son was the groom. It was creative, elegant, and beautiful.

Brigid on the other hand, knew that she didn't want to be the typical bride. She didn't know what she wanted, but she knew what she didn't want. In planning, she wanted something truly unique that reflected her Irish heritage. She contacted the costumers from the Renaissance Fair where she had participated in several years of summer acting. They provided her with an authentic Renaissance 1600's period gown made up of five pieces overlaying each other. Her groom wore a morning coat with spats. Brigid didn't want to wear a veil because that would not have been true to the period, but she introduced a train to the dress. She incorporated several Irish traditions into their wedding. The bride's bouquet included a St. Brigid's cross (the word "bride" is a nickname for St. Brigid) and a horseshoe. The bridal party's bouquets included Hydrangeas (devotion), Bells of Ireland (whimsy), Ferns (sincerity) and Ivy (wedded love.) The bridal colors represented the ancient Irish flag's colors of blue and gold while her gown was white. On Brigid's wedding bouquet were bells to represent an ancient Irish belief that ringing bells wards away the evil faeries. The guests were asked that in lieu of rice or birdseed, the guests would ring bells to greet the bride and groom.

Following a church wedding, the reception was held outdoors in the Bridgewater, Connecticut Town pavilion. It was creative, simple, and beautiful.

1) Both brides knew what they didn't want in this time of celebration. Consequently, each planned a wedding that beautifully portrayed their personality. Does your Christmas celebration include traditions and decorations that reflect your heritage? Will your children know and appreciate what these items are and why they are important to you?

2) Has your celebration become so overloaded with traditions that there is no time for anything new? or a time for silence? Is there something you should let go of? Is there a tradition that taxes your time and resources and really has little meaning left besides the fact that you have always done it that way?

Brigid's wedding and Renaissance gown. Eileen, Joe, Brigid, Tim

Ashley's wishbook wedding: Derek, Melody, Vance, Ashley, Brenda and Justin

Christmas Countdown, 2004

From Eileen:

We started getting into the winter mode on November 12, 2004, when we had our first snowfall of the season. Has someone moved Connecticut further north when we weren't looking? The cold is giving us a good excuse to sit by the fire and mellow out with thoughts of friends, family, and Christmases past. . .and to reflect on how life has changed for us this year. . .

Brett continues his adventure in Appalachia School of Law—halfway done (done being our favorite word.) To his credit, his grades reflect his serious and lengthy study hours. He has even managed in his down time to locate a product liability case which may still be going long after he passes the bar.

Joe has kissed his long commute goodbye again and put himself full time into his Supply Chain consulting business. Happily, SCS has proven to be more than enough to keep him busy. He now commutes to his office upstairs with occasional trips out of town to see clients.

Eileen hasn't killed him yet, so we think this arrangement will work out!

Brigid has had an amazing year, her wedding to Tim Carney being the high point. Oct 9th was the prettiest and most emotional day of the Fall. Having loved ones around for such a moment had our tear ducts working on overdrive. She and Tim left for a honeymoon in Rome and returned to continue their hard work in getting their business, Carney Home Enterprises, off the ground. They have enough projects on the calendar to keep them hopping for some time. If you need some home re-hab, we'll put a good word in for you—we know the owners.

Eileen has elementary, middle, and high school students this year, so she finds herself bouncing from school to school. They are great kids! Her Women's Guild held their annual Craft Fair in November, so her kiln was cooking for most of the summer and Fall. Joe bought Eileen a new potter's wheel this summer, but things have been too frantic for any creativity in that direction. But NEXT year....!

In the meantime, Brenda reports:

Stuff that scares us and then we're blessed!

John was diagnosed with prostate cancer in February. Who would believe that a second husband in his 50's would be pestered by the big C. However, John came through the cryoablation surgery like a champ and was back on the golf course and work in two weeks' time. This is a new technological treatment, so we're blessed!

I was laid off my job in August as Senior VP Consultant by a downsizing event. The longer you investigate the future, the shorter you have to get things accomplished, so I've been examining what I really want to do. To lose a job can be a blessing! I came up with two thoughts. I have been feeling a little micromanaged in the last company--so I want to work for a company so huge that nobody who works there knows what it does, and it pays big bucks while appreciating my talents. Or my ideal is I'll land a job where I nurture talent development and innovation with enlightened leaders, a concept not easily found! The search is on!

Derek has found Las Vegas or vice versa. He is an entrepreneur who promotes night clubs. At 29, he has gained a contract at Mandarin Bay for their Friday night promotion. Melody has been promoted to Assistant Manager of a small retail store. I thought I would make some purchases in her store, but somehow, I'm in between Granny Chic and uncomfortable conversations with salesclerks whose low-rise jeans don't quite rise enough for me. I can't help but send secret looks at the navel jewelry or tattoos. Melody, though, looks terrific.

Justin has just completed his MBA at 27. Like me, he is expecting prospective employers to catch fire, burning for his expertise. He informs me for Christmas he is part of the iPod generation (a hint). In this speeded up generation, he runs 4-5 miles daily to counteract stress. It looks good on him—when I go to the gym, I push the carb burner dial on the treadmill, burn 120 calories and stop for a smoothie when I'm finished. Have you tried Cardio kick boxing and aqua challenge where you groove it, move it and ride in high gear on a bike? Unfortunately, even yoga basics remain a humiliating experience for me. I'm sticking to the cardio dance classes.

Vance is not to be outdone. He is working on his second year of his MBA at TCU and enjoying the thrills of a graduate assistantship, full time MBA program and 20-hour internship. Ashley packs his lunch for him. His keyboard needs to feature a toaster-oven-style crumb tray because he's either driving to school or working projects. Ashley continues her job as pre-school teacher at Lamplighter School in Dallas. She is a planner and has a well-deserved graduation trip to Europe for the two of them in May. It is already fully planned.

Skylar, at five years has started kindergarten and lost her two front teeth in time for Christmas. While reading with her on her computer lap-style book, I commented that when I was a girl, books didn't talk with us and ask questions aloud. She shook her head in complete disbelief. Thinking about this, techies have run amok with our books—why don't they make smart clothes, so your bra knows when your chest sags and gives it an on-the-spot lift? In the meantime, Skylar and I are enjoying the wonders of talking books.

So yes, we've had scares, but dreams have soared to their potential!

Let's Discuss:

1) This year has brought job loss or changes for us. Have you turned your career over to the Lord? If so, how has your understanding of His guidance evolved?

2) Meditate on Psalm 23 today (The Lord is my Shepherd; I shall not want). Have you seen or felt the Lord's presence in your life as a shepherd?

3) At Christmas, we gain a new appreciation for shepherds. After all, angels appeared to them. Later, Jesus asked Peter, "Do you love me?" and Peter replied, "Lord, you know I do." Jesus responded, "Feed my sheep." Have you thought about your place as a shepherd or your place as a sheep?

   Eileen had a modern-day example of her priest saying, "I don't know of any shepherds, do you?" Joe sheepishly put his hand up. (He owned a dozen sheep with Madonna as the chief sheep after the dearly departed Kramer). So, the priest continued his sermon, "Besides Joe, we don't know any shepherds today." Are you a shepherd or a sheep?

4) The Gospel says that the shepherds went in haste to Bethlehem where they found Mary, Joseph, and Jesus. The shepherds *moved* toward Christ. Our life has a movement and flow, never standing still. We can direct where our life is headed, or we can drift. Have you thought lately about which direction your life is moving—toward Christ or adrift? It is moving one direction or another. Being stationery is moving backward.

Christmas Countdown, 2005

Hope you are in a holiday mood and getting ready for the best year ever! The Buchheit clan has had an eventful year and we're ready for more!

Brett is in his last year of Law School and will take the Bar Exam in 2006. He's had an amazing- and exhausting- experience. Send along your good thoughts for his results! In his "free time" this fall, he organized a group to collect thousands of pounds of food for Katrina evacuees. He's still working on a class action suit for a friend who was injured loading an off-track vehicle onto a ramp. Last, but not least, there's still a chance he'll be running for the Mayor of Grundy this spring- a politician in the family?! We'll let you know ALL the results next Christmas!

Brigid and Tim are doing well. She has established herself in Real Estate – very hot in Litchfield County. She's decided to run for "Mrs. Connecticut"- a surefire way to establish client recognition?! She, too, took part in events to help hurricane victims, notably as the organizer and M.C. of a talent show sponsored by her church. (She even got her mother to make her debut in "stand up" comedy- no fruit was thrown!) Tim's business of bustling rehabbing and renovating jobs are backed up four months. Needless to say, "This Old House" is required viewing around here! Tim has become a real "Bridgewatonian" - he was the Tractor Parade judge this year and, surprisingly, our float won a medal- do I hear snickering out there?!

Joe continues in defense consulting (Supply Chain Solution, LLC) and recruiting (Academy Associates) while still enjoying the "commute" from the bedroom to his newly renovated office upstairs, but some of his clients have him flying back and forth to D.C. on a far too regular basis. That being the exception, it's nice to have a coffee break together when Eileen comes home from school! She has yet another new student- all from the same family. They seem to come every year or so – thus ensuring her retirement in six years or so when they finally run out of family members!

We built the "Great Wall of Bridgewater" this year- an 80-foot stone wall along the road in front of the house, constructed by a merry band of Ecuadorians who took our ideas and changed them – dramatically. The result – long in coming- is different from our original idea, but it's growing on us... and, with around twenty pallets of stone and six tons of cement, it's not going anywhere.

In a year where weather was often a major news item, we learned our lesson and made our first New Year's Resolution- no more trips to the Yucatan during hurricane season. "Stanley" (my grandfather's name no less) was with us in Cancun and, while we didn't have to evacuate, we were "forced:" to rest and relax, thanks to the wind and rain. (Not a bad thing, just not what we had in mind.) I choose to think that Stanley was saving me from being eaten by a Great White by keeping my buns out of the water!

There's always room for you here- come for a visit! (Bring carrots and you'll make friends forever in the pasture!) All our best for a happy and healthy new year-

While Eileen was learning about imperfection of Mother Nature and a merry band of Ecuadorians, Brenda was examining imperfection from another angle.

From Brenda: You, like me, may have decided to take the easy way out. This great event in our lives is the decision to forego the annual trek to find the perfect Christmas tree. We always made this trip on what turned out to be the coldest weather day, so we would shiver as we vainly looked to see if the tree trunk's curvature was too obviously out of whack. Getting that tree on the car roof was another story. We thought we had to wait until about 2 weeks before Christmas, so the tree would be as fresh as possible. Waiting those two weeks in Texas weather meant going from an amiable 60 degrees to another drop of ten to twenty degrees of cold. Well, that freshness theory was shot out of the water when I read that the Christmas tree harvest begins in the middle of summer. No wonder our living room floor would be covered with needles despite our attempt for freshness!

Also, it was a very strange coincidence. Allergies would strike several members of the family. We finally figured out that the culprit was cedar pine trees. We switched from natural to prelit. Our new tree isn't fragrant with the lovely Christmas smell of evergreen. Its prelit beauty is far more sparkling than the former wrestled trees from parking lot to twining & winding Christmas lights among pine needles, . . .but it is like a person with a face lift—pretty but lacking the evidence of living. Our tree needs to have a few branches out of sync to show that it has weathered a few storms. It needs to smell of the earth, the rain, the sticky sap of its existence. On the other hand, flicking the lights with a switch is terrific. Our new tree is a product of man's creation. God must smile as he watches us. He may wonder why it takes us so long to discover that the beauty that delights and holds our attention is not found in perfection, but in just the right dash of imperfection.

So, where is the beauty and delight in our family? Vance completed his MBA at Texas Christian University in May and had a job immediately following graduation. He and Ashley celebrated with their first trip to Europe. The imperfection? Ooops. The carefully and joyfully taken photos got lost in a camera—that was accidentally left on the plane. The pictures remain lost.

Justin completed his MBA at Southern Methodist University and has a job beginning in 2006 with Deutsch Bank in Dallas. Derek and Melody are happy in Las Vegas, with Skylar taking first grade by storm and she really loves to read.

So where is the imperfection? I'm sad to say that the "other woman" called in October to let me know that she and my husband have been having an affair for the last two years of our three-year marriage—a soap opera pales in comparison. She said she got tired of men lying to women, so she wanted to let me know. That's another reason why an easier, convenient, and less aggravating tree is so appealing to me to put up this year.

And here's a riddle. What is green, covered in tinsel, and goes ribbet, ribbet. It's a mistle-toad. Or perhaps it is a husband whose lover just revealed their affair. And speaking of imperfection, there is the first couple in the Bible. This reminds me of another riddle: What did Adam say to Eve, the night before Christmas?

"It's Christmas, Eve. "Of course, she responded by whacking him with the apple. I have thought of some whacking myself.

Let's Discuss:

1) There comes a time when our children or grandchildren will question Santa Claus. There also comes a time when God uses us to reach out and restore belief in Him. We do this by showing others Christ when all else points to doubt. When has reason or doubt tried to cloud your spiritual vision? Have you helped others with their doubts?

2) What helped restore your real sight or insight? If not restored, what would help you? What are some steps that need to be taken?

3) We live in an imperfect world. Have you been able to find the beauty in imperfection?

4) Sometime, even though Eileen and I are doing our best, things don't go as we want them to go. There are a lot of things we can't control. We question ourselves: Have I done my best? Is this my fault, someone else's fault or 50/50? All we can do is rest assured that God will be at our side, no matter what. Sometimes we must allow others to love us, without demanding that they fully understand us. And sometimes we must be willing to do the same for others.

Christmas Countdown, 2006

From Eileen: We have a lot to celebrate this year! It all started when Brett brought in 2006 by asking Leslie Craft to be his wife! (If you hear cheering in the background, it's us!) Leslie is a wonderful girl. We love her AND she puts up with Brett!

Spring brought Brett's graduation from Law School. We rented the world's largest RV and drove to Appalachia with Grandpa. (Go and rent the Robin Williams film and imagine our faces.) Arriving in "Greater Grundy", we were greeted by the town's billboard saying, "Welcome Maw and Paw Buchheit"! We soon found that Brett was known and loved by many- old ladies in tears told us how much he'd be missed. (We're pretty sure they weren't bribed.)At graduation, he was inducted into Who's Who, earned the "Book Award" and a humanitarian award. We were soooo proud! The icing on the cake was our chance to get to know Leslie's parents – lovely people who put up with Brett, too!

Brigid and Tim bought a house in Bridgewater in April. It is soooo nice to have them close by! Brigid's year as "Mrs. Bridgewater" included two pageants- one in which she convinced her husband and her dad and about twenty other grown men to dress in drag and vie for "Miss Bridgewater" (neither of our guys won- go figure.) The state contest brought her "Mrs. Congeniality" and the "Spirit Award"- an amazing finish to her reign! This fall marked a new beginning for the Carney Clan-
A first grandbaby will be born in June! To say that we're excited is the understatement of all time! If we time this right, Brigid could give birth at Brett's wedding!!!

As the summer closed, Brett and Leslie packed up and moved to New Orleans, Louisiana, where Brett will earn his LLM at Tulane. Finding a place to live and a job for Leslie proved to be a challenge, but they pulled it off. We have hopes of visiting them there before they move – again. (This must be hereditary.)

So, as Christmas comes closer, Tim's business continues to flourish, and Brigid is selling houses in an economy where they're not supposed to be selling. Brett is studying like mad, and Leslie is teaching in a Catholic school. Joe's consulting work keeps him busy, with trips and travels to all points (including the upstairs office!). Eileen's ESL students are still giving her a reason to get up and go every morning. And we're all looking forward to spring!

From Brenda: Here's a Charles Dickens thought!

Christmas brings great expectations.

Derek just brought in 5 boxes of 300 net lights saying, "This year, let's do those big trees out front." If you've noticed a large glow in the sky, we are dancing with visions of the Griswolds in our head.

Further great expectations meant Spring Cleaning was interesting. I swept a husband out the door. (The divorce was final in February.) Being single brings bittersweet discoveries: loneliness yet completion; fear yet liberation; opportunities yet challenges. I did a lifelong dream. In June, I taught a three week "Cross Cultural Management" course at Russian American Christian University in Moscow. Not speaking the language, traveling on my own, staying at a Russian provided apartment was a gift from God. Only He could have arranged that one! It was on an "arranged date" (arranged by mutual friends) that I heard about the opportunity in Russia. The "date" wasn't a mutual thrill, but the opportunity was! I donated my vacation time from my full-time job at Bell Helicopter to go over in June. It was such a good experience that I have agreed to donate my time again next summer.

Another wonderful opportunity has popped up. Derek and Melody have decided to move their family from Las Vegas. It is closer to me. They have taken the 3 empty bedrooms upstairs! I love it! Skylar can walk to second grade at the local top ranked elementary school. She is learning to ride her bike on the trails by my home. Derek wants to remain in night club promotion but in the Dallas scene.

Justin has been selected as an officer of Idlewild, the 100-year-old debutante social club in Dallas. This means he is “networking” up close and personal in the “Season.” He continues to work in Real Estate Development for Deutsche Bank.

Vance has just started a new job in real estate development with a Dallas company while Ashley continues to teach at Lamplighter School in Dallas.

The media delivers one dire message after another. . .global warming, oil shortage, hordes of illegal immigrants, bird flu, Al Qaeda. . .It is information and worry overload. We are lulled into a false security, assuming that our near future will be more of the same present.

How stunned we are when a stone or boulder plops into our placid life pond. The splash and rippling effect of the event touches us in many ways: a knot in the stomach, clammy hands, rapid heartbeat, inexplicable sudden tears, the inability to focus on the task at hand. I have experienced them all. Even when the event is in the past, the symptoms can remain. We are haunted with whys and what ifs. This seems magnified when it is a loss, such as a divorce or death.

The truth is that we never did possess the ability to handle or control the future. The future has tantalizing or terrifying hints from shadows. We can’t hurry the future. We can’t see into its hidden days. Yet, we forge ahead, dreaming, making plans, planting trees that we may not live to see reach maturity. The stomach unknots, and the heartbeat slows to a normal rhythm as we realize that our God will give us the wisdom and strength to deal with the present, the ripples and waves in our pond. We call this

Mindfulness—living in the present and slowly breathing in and out. And so, the healing begins.

Let's talk:

1) Christ's birth is more than just a story; it is history that should drastically alter the way we live our lives. If we fully internalize the birth of the one "who came to destroy the one who has the power of death," it should completely shift the paradigm through which we view and live life. Do you feel the freedom to pursue a healthy life? What is obstructing that life?

2) Have you downplayed the birth of Jesus to be just a story rather than the ultimate gift of freedom? How can you remind yourself that Jesus' birth is much more than just a story?

3) Is God encouraging you to share this message of freedom with anyone today? Name them!

4) "Rejoice in the Lord always; again I will say, Rejoice" Philippians 4:4. This seems like an unrealistic expectation that Paul gives to the church in Philippi. Life is full of ups and downs. Can people rejoice in moments of darkness? Paul is saying **Rejoice in the Lord** always. Though circumstances will change, the Lord is consistent. Can you have hardships without becoming hard? Heartbreaks without being broken? Can you take a deep breath slowly in and let go slowly out?

Christmas Countdown, 2007

From Eileen: all the amazing things that happened this year, we'll follow the seasons and tell you the stories!

Winter brought plans for Brett and Leslie's wedding and a Novena for good weather in June for their garden reception. Brigid and Tim were in "waiting mode" as her pregnancy progressed, with her due date and the wedding running neck and neck.

Spring brought Brett's graduation from Tulane and an LLM to add to the list of alphabets following his name. Last minute details for the wedding – baby and vows still set for the same date.

June brought relatives and friends to Connecticut, getting ready for the big day, June 9th. Obviously, the baby didn't want to miss a good party because, at almost midnight on D-Day, June 6th, she decided enough was enough. Our granddaughter, Flynn Ayers Carney, was named after the Gaelic "Flynn", meaning "child of the red headed warrior" and "Ayers" for all the Irish relatives on my grandfather's side. She missed the wedding, but she had a chance to stay with her Grandma Carney so her parents could make the ceremony.

All of you who are grandparents know the amazing joy you feel- try mixing it with a wedding! No, on second thought, DON'T! It's an emotional overload! Since Joe was the officiating Justice of the Peace, my worry was not blubbering out loud throughout the ceremony! A perfect day!

Summer brought "house arrest" for me. After nearly a year of pulmonary problems, my doctor made me stay away from germy people and germy places. Once school was out, I was in- literally. Six weeks later, we saw that the doctor wasn't nuts and that going back to teaching was an invitation to the ER.

So, fall brought retirement. Babysitting a few times a week and my women's guild activities have filled things in nicely! Joe continues consulting work but is spending more time on recruiting and less time in airports, a welcome relief! Playing with Flynn rounds things out perfectly! Here's hoping that you and yours are having a happy, healthy holiday!

From Brenda:

Great expectations have arrived at the Shull house also! Ashley and Vance have found out that they will be bringing Mary Craddock Shull into the world next Spring. Save the date as I'm sure a permanent smile will have to be surgically removed from all! The nursery is painted a shell pink, the bed bundled in pink and green with the crowning touch of a small white chandelier. It's a room fit for a tiny princess! Right now, all is calm. All is bright. Ashley already has it picture perfect with Vance's painting arm a little bruised!

Derek is launching a business called The Guest List book, an online book of nightclubs with discounts available—with a few up and running issues, it should be in working order soon. Melody has been Homeroom Mother or as she calls it "Skylar's Life Assistant" this year. Skylar is a gifted 3rd grader winning reading awards. She just finished book 6 of Harry Potter, having started the hefty volume series six months ago. She is now into the book for Daring Girls and wants to have a "spy" party for her 9th birthday.

Justin has been selected Vice President of Idlewild, the 100-year-old debutante social club in Dallas. This takes up most of his social focus. It is rumored he will be selected as President next. He continues to work in real estate development at Deutsche Bank.

Let's Talk:

1) Lots of job changes occurred this year for the Shull's and Buchheits. What is God calling you to do? Take time to pray about the things, both big and small, that God has called you to do recently.

2) Are you ready? Pray to God and ask for the boldness to do the things God has called you to do, knowing that God has called you and prepared you for the task.

3) A friend of Eileen's said, "I'm too old to wear tight shoes." This philosophy does not only apply to footwear. It goes to any project you will never complete. Any book you can't seem to get through. Any irritation that absolutely won't change. Can you name some tasks that you should just "Let it go?" so that you can get to the ones God is calling you to do? Have you prioritized your Christmas list by recognizing there are some things that you need to just let it go?

Christmas Countdown, 2008

From Eileen: There were lots of changes in our lives in 2008 – still waiting for the part where life "slows down". We seem to speed up!

Brett and Leslie are enjoying Denver. In Buchheit fashion, they have already moved into another house! It's a great neighborhood and close to their jobs. Brett's practicing with a firm and still writing law articles. He's been published in an international law review and has an additional grant for writing a research paper. Leslie gave the office world a try but her true love is teaching and she's back in the classroom again. She missed it and she's good at it–can't beat that combination!

Brigid, Tim and Flynn made a major move - to Rochester, New York. That's Tim's old stomping ground and his family lives nearby. The catalyst was a job offer from the not-for-profit Blue Cross/Blue Shield for Brigid. With the real estate market going nowhere, it was too good to refuse. Tim was ready for a change, too. Being his own boss was liberating – and exhausting! They've sold their house here in Bridgewater and are getting ready to put Tim's skills to good use rehabbing their next place. Flynn keeps us all running -literally. That girl never did walk when she could run! What a joy!

Joe is still making the "long" commute to his office upstairs with

periodic breaks for espresso. He's doing less traveling and more computing-LOTS more computing! The animals keep him busy, and he keeps coming up with projects which take on a life force all their own. The latest is a parking pad next to the driveway-you'll have to see it for yourselves... when it gets done...

After a six-month attempt at being the director of our town's seniors' group, planning activities and writing the newsletter, I am, once again, happily unemployed. I found that I was allergic to...bureaucracy. It was "a bad fit". Now, I'm slowly but surely working my way through half mished projects and "stuff' with the goal of being able to pick up and travel at will-like to Denver or upstate New York!

From Brenda:
I am happy to announce that the Shull family welcomed Mary Craddock Shull. It was a little earlier than expected, but it was a very healthy and happy delivery that father, uncle, both grandparents and friends attended. Mary Craddock is tiny but thriving. Her name is bigger than she is!

This reminded me of one of the favorite books I used to read when the boys were babies. It is called *"I Love You Forever."* Let's get to the ending:

Well, that mother, she got older. She got older and older and older. One day she called up her son and said, "You'd better come see me because I'm very old and sick." So her son came to see her. When he came in the door, she tried to sing the song. She sang ***I'll love you forever, I'll like you for always. . .*** *but she couldn't finish because she was too old and sick. The son went to his mother. He picked her up and rocked her back and forth, back, and forth, back, and forth. And he sang this song: "****I'll love you forever, I'll like you for always, As long as I'm living, my***

Mother you'll be. *When the son came home that night, he stood for a long time at the top of the stairs. Then he went into the room where his very new baby daughter was sleeping. He picked her up in his arms and very slowly rocked her back and forth, back, and forth, back, and forth. And while he rocked her, he sang I'll* ***love you forever, I'll like you for always, As long as I'm living my baby you'll be."***

Don't you wonder sometimes about the joyful reality that our Heavenly Father feels that way about us. . .and will love us forever and like us for always.

Let's Talk:

1) British actor Jeremy Irons once said, "We all have our time machines. Some take us back, they're called memories. Some take us forward, they're called dreams." It seems the birth of babies evoke memories and dreams in a life cycle. Have you experienced this looking forward and looking back? Have you experienced that Christmas is a time of looking forward and looking back?

2) Do you believe that one of the purposes of good memories is the anticipation of creating new ones? Why or why not?

3) What activity for you at Christmas fills this season with joy, a happiness that makes us feel warm in our hearts?

Christmas Countdown, 2009

From Eileen: The temperature is falling, and the sky looks threatening—a white Christmas may be right around the corner!

It seemed like we spent much of 2009 in transit. There were trips to Rochester to visit Brigid, Tim and Flynn. Is there anything better than being a grandparent? In our roles as "Nonna" and "Lo Stello", aka Grandpa, we relish our time together. . .and with Flynn's parents, too. We also made a trip to Richmond, Va., to visit our old friends from Germany, the Thomassons.

We added 2 more rescues to our menagerie. Sinbad-the-Cat joined us from a rescue that was about to euthanize him for an "out of control" condition. He was so stressed out at the shelter that a friend asked us to give it a try since she knew we had been down this road before. He is now the premiere barn cat at Fair View Farm and in constant need of attention. He has earned his keep as a mighty hunter and if he continues to pull his weight, he's a keeper! No one comes to the house that isn't greeted by Sinbad. Petting is optional.

Also, Danny Boy, a 2 ½ yr old Lab something mix, has joined us in June. Similar story but we were much more cautious with an indoor pet. Danny had been so neglected; he didn't know how to play. Now you can't stop him. He is also a welcome addition.

Joe's dad has become a Connecticut resident since around June this year after a brief illness. He relocated to a wonderful place in Bethel only 8 minutes from our house. He is doing exceptionally well and continues to adjust to the rigorous life of having everything done for him including meals, laundry, and weekly visits from us. We now have a new standard for senior living. It is as close to nirvana as you could get. The transition was arduous, and Joe has decided to write a book on the experience. As he said, "No one should have to go through this twice!" and he is hoping to develop it as a guidebook.

We had a great family reunion in August, just in time for the annual Bridgewater Country Fair. Brett and Leslie flew in from Denver to join the rest of the clan, including GG or Great Grandpa (Joe's dad). They are now the proud parents of a black lab named Moose—do we see a pattern here?

Brigid is now a full-fledged Program Manager having passed certification this year and has been chosen to foster several new projects at Blue Cross/Blue Shield of Rochester. She's on to her MBA in the next few years. Tim landed a great position with the NY School System as Master Cabinet Teacher at the hugely successful BOCES program. We are hoping for a relocation to something closer to us but have discovered AMTRAK as a great way to travel.

Brett is burning the midnight oil at his Law Firm and loving it. Seventy plus hours a week and he is still wildly excited by the profession. Leslie continues to teach in a year-round elementary school program, 9 weeks on, 3 weeks off. Seems to fit well!

From Brenda:

The year 2009 brought a stock market tumble and strong unemployment dip starting in November. Somehow, after three years on the market, my home sold in October! This means I missed the stock market tumble by one month! Plus, I had three weeks to move, downsizing from 5000 sq. ft to a 2300 sq. ft townhouse in West Highland Park. I moved the day before Thanksgiving. However, I was able to have Thanksgiving dinner with all the family in attendance at my new townhouse. The biggest attraction is that my new town home is 4 minutes from Vance and Ashley (or more specifically from 2.5 yrs. old Mary Craddock).

My 85-year-old father, who had come out of remission from non-Hodgkin's lymphoma after 24 years, has successfully once again beaten the disease. Of course, at 85 he dozes off at strange moments while we watch Mary Craddock play. This is a huge puzzle to Mary Craddock because she hates naps! She stops playing and walks up to him, staring in disbelief and touches his knee. He, of course, claims he was not dozing in the chair, just thinking with his eyes shut

All these above-named events were smoke signals!

See what you think. Here is the story. The only survivor of a shipwreck washed up on a small, uninhabited island. He prayed feverishly for God to rescue him and every day he scanned the horizon for help. None seemed forthcoming. Exhausted, he eventually managed to build a little hut out of driftwood to protect him from the elements and to store his few possessions. But then one day, after scavenging for food, he arrived home to find his little hut in flames. The smoke rolled up to the sky. The worst had happened; everything was lost.

He was stunned with grief and anger. "God, how could you do this to me!" he cried. Early the next day, however, he was awakened by the sound of a ship that was approaching the island. It had come to rescue him. “How did you know I was here?” asked the weary man of his rescuers. “We saw your smoke signal, “they replied.

We get discouraged when things are not looking good or not being what we planned. But God is at work in our lives, even amid pain and suffering or bringing joy when it looks like disaster. We become discouraged when our Christmas plans start falling apart or our careful plans disintegrate before our very eyes.

Remember, the next time your little hut is burning to the ground—it may be a smoke signal that summons the grace of God.

You say: It is impossible! God says: All things are possible (Luke 18:27)

You say: I cannot go on! God says: My grace is sufficient (2 Corinthians 23:9)

Let’s Talk:

1) What are some smoke signals in your life? How has God answered in the past?

2) How are you looking for Jesus this Christmas? Is he part of a smoke signal answer for the future?

3) Have you experienced the real smoke signals with a ruined Turkey or Christmas dish? Did something turn out better?

Christmas Countdown, 2010

From Eileen: Once again, we've gone through many changes. We downsized in January. No, not moving again! After a nasty fall in January, Joe decided it was time to only have animals that are mostly self-sufficient. That is, can make it to the pasture fence without his help! We're down to a donkey and a miniature horse, both males. That said, our "inside" numbers increased when the Guiding Eyes for the Blind called to say our long awaited "release" dog (translate—not too bright) was available. Thomas Jefferson (their call) rapidly became T.J and has been a welcome, if somewhat goofy addition.

In the spring, Eileen got word that a book she'd been working on was accepted by the publishers. Along with a friend from Roxbury, she's writing a pictorial history of our two towns. With some technical help from Joe (since the word pixel now drives Eileen up the wall), the pictures' scans and narratives are becoming reality! With luck, the final draft will go to the editor this month, to the printer in January and finally be in print come spring.

Brigid, Tim, and Flynn came for the Bridgewater Fair in August. While telecommuting, Brigid found out that she had gotten a promotion. The only condition was that she live near a branch. Would you believe there was one in Connecticut? They were moved by month's end—into a house across the street from the one they left two years ago. Even though Tim had a wonderful year teaching at the vocational school, the budget wasn't going to guarantee him a slot this semester. In the meantime, word went out that he is back and folks are lining up to have him fix their houses—nice to be loved! We are thrilled to have them back in the "hood." Meanwhile, Flynn is getting to be a Big Girl. That means Nursery School three days a week and Nonna's house two afternoons a week. Who could be happier?

Brett and Leslie experienced major changes, too. They found their third, and hopefully, last house in Denver's Washington Park neighborhood. This may be the one they buy. Leslie must have been in the military in a former life, as she brings these moves off like a pro. Brett has opened his own practice. What an accomplishment! We are so pleased. God knows there was a lot of arduous work to make all this so!

Joe keeps holding down the fort. His recruiting business proves that there really are jobs out there, even in this economy. He continues to commute to the office upstairs lucky for Eileen, so he can work two jobs at the same time.

From Brenda:

June 2010 found me in Bethlehem, looking at the exact place that it is believed that the baby Jesus was born. This was a trip to Israel with a Sunday School class that had been planned for two years. It was such a moving experience to be in the olive grove of the garden of Gethsemane where the actual olive trees of Jesus time are still alive due to the ability of those trees to be alive for several thousand years. This trip made the Bible come alive!

Lo and behold, the very same day I was in Bethlehem, Vance and Ashley were giving birth to my third granddaughter! They named her Evelyn Lee Shull. Vance gave her David's middle name of Lee to honor his dad. Last Sunday I attended Evelyn's baptism and she is, of course, a beautiful baby! I have told her I rode a camel in her honor on the day of her birth (which is a bumpy, joggling journey—I called my camel "Humperdink. I don't think that is its Arabic name.) I don't recommend camel rides. When they get up and down, it is a long jig swaying and jiggling way up there!

Since my management consulting has "considerably slowed," a polite phrase for unemployment in this economically challenged year following the stock market drop, I was able to spend the month of May in Lithuania teaching an undergraduate business course at a Christian university (LCC International University). Earlier I had visited Joe and Carol Shull who live in Washington, D.C. I was delighted that they were able to meet me to do sightseeing in Lithuania while I was teaching there.

July brought an opportunity to go on an Alaskan cruise to celebrate the surprise engagement of a friend/couple. In great secrecy, he planned to give her some ice (diamond engagement ring) on the ice. We secretly got to tag along. Wouldn't you know that the helicopter to take them to the glacier was grounded by the wind, but the proposal went well. She said yes.

After reading "Eat, Pray, Love", I found an inexpensive last minute September excursion to Thailand to travel by myself. For me it was "Eat, Pray, Eat." This time I rode friendly Asian elephants. I have pictures of camel and elephant rides for those of you who doubt! I know. I know. This sounds like shades of Auntie Mame and impossible to believe with five trips in close succession.

So yes, 2010 has been an amazing year. More than I could envision from riding camels to Asian elephants!! Mission opportunities brought the Baltic and Israel with last minute, incredibly inexpensive trips to Alaska and Thailand. New paths, new journey, lots of blessings! Quite a contrast to previous years.

Let's Talk:

1) What are some examples of the work that Jesus has left for us until he comes again? On both a global level and personal level what is work for you to do?

2) Buchheit offspring experienced moves to familiar areas. You may not have experienced a physical move this Christmas. However, can you relate to becoming so familiar with a person, relationship or even Christmas that you fail to fully appreciate its truth? Does familiarity overshadow its worth? Is there a way to look at it with a new perspective or energy?

Christmas Countdown, 2011

From Brenda:

I think it's good to write Christmas cards. It's kind of like New Year's resolutions. You look back over the year and think of the highlights that bump you along your life's journey. You'll see our family is growing. Those frenetic jostling of 3 sons when we entered a room or knocking /pushing each other when I tried to check out in the grocery line have softened. I now have 3 granddaughters who want me to shop, play hide & seek, rock them, or retrieve a blankie. Skylar, a budding 7th grader, ran for student council president, is in Honor Society & tried out for girls' basketball. Melody and Derek had moved from my home three years ago to live near Austin. Derek continues entrepreneurial pursuits.

Vance and Ashley have a toddler, Evelyn at 16 mos. This is a child who favors you with her blankie or shakes her head no when she means yes. She is busy copying Mary Craddock's ballet moves. Mary Craddock at 3.5 years knows how to negotiate what she clearly wants, was dressed as a Spanish flamenco dancer for Halloween, and is conversant both with a ballet plié or soccer hustle. Vance and

Ashley sold their home in August to move 6 blocks to a lovelier home and different school district. It's the exact same excellent elementary school Ashley attended as a child!

Justin also is being initiated into the world of taxes and lawncare. However, his first bachelor home has a hot tub and outdoor patio complete with television. Somehow, he and Vance are close in neighborhoods, but far apart in equipping their houses!

If you look closely at me, you'll see that I have morphed. The Lord has been moving down my check list. I went to Spain and Portugal in the Spring (hence Mary Craddock's Halloween costume). I worked with HIV orphans in Africa in June with a side trip to Scotland. In July I taught at the University of Guilin in China, and I return on mission trip to China in 2 months, teaching some seminars in Beijing and Anchon. I taught an MBA class at the University of Dallas this Fall.

Strangely enough it has come to me in several events and Bible verses that the best thing for me is to learn to be still and hear the Lord passing. I'm learning it is in the quiet not the roar of these lovely Christmas nights. Whenever we are out driving and see the Christmas lights, may they call to mind to me and you the One who brings the light to our darkness. Yep! It's quite a journey! May God who called us to live in hope and expectation go with you!

For the Buchheits, 2011 was a year of "beginnings" and they took many forms. On October 29th, we welcomed Amelia Rose Buchheit, who weighed in at 7lb. 14 oz. Her proud parents, Leslie and Brett, have sore cheeks from all the smiling, as do her grandparents on both sides. We made a trip to Denver to meet her on November 13th and loved every minute—especially the snuggles and smooches.

Eileen became a published author with the completion of "Images of America—Roxbury and Bridgewater," one of the Arcadia's series of histories told through photography. (If you're curious, go to www.arcadiapublishing.com) Joe supplied the technical savvy to make the images come alive. Her co-author, Jeannine Green, had the patience and publishing experience to bring it all together.

Brigid and Tim's house was hit by not one, not two, but three flying trees in a freak storm this spring, resulting in extensive damage to the roof. Making lemonade out of lemons, they are planning to put on an additional floor before replacing the roof!!

Flynn continues to delight and amaze us. Do we sound like grandparents? She spent the summer swimming in the pool with "Stello" and supervising the workers at both locations—sound like anyone you know? Now at four, she's a "big girl," deep into pre-reading, being a princess and soaking up the world around her.

Joe expanded his horizons by helping Tim build the Waldorf Astoria of chicken houses in the back yard. It's color coordinated to match the barn! Two Guinea hens patrol the grounds—often crossing the street to visit the neighbors—we've been down this path before—and have the phone number of the poultry supplier on speed dial to replace "missing" or "nearsighted" hens. Joe worked this summer with Tim on our house repairs from winter snow damage, proving that even an experienced logistician is no match for the inefficiency of local hardware stores. Our favorite word was—and is- "done". . .which we are not. Wishing you every joy and Christmas blessing—come and meet the chicken girls in their Waldorf.

Let's Discuss:

From the roar of a winter storm, to the soft "no that means yes," it is the quiet not the roar of these winter nights that truly brings the message of Christmas.

1Kings 19:12 says "After the earthquake came a fire, but the Lord was not in the fire. And after the fire came a gentle whisper."

1) Have you allowed for a time of quiet and rest so that it can become clear to you what your strength and passion is? How have you taken the time to listen?
   It was prayer time, and I was putting my sons to bed. I said cheerfully to my son Justin who was seven, "Justin, wasn't today wonderful?" Then I listed the litany of things we had done on that Saturday (his soccer game, watching a TCU basketball game and a movie that night). He nodded, but in a sweet small voice he said, "Yes, but I didn't get to play." Even at seven, he missed the time to refuel. I listened. I learned. I found out not to pack a heavy schedule on him at an early age.

2) Is your Christmas an earthquake or a gentle whisper?

Christmas Countdown, 2012

From Brenda:

I decided to go a different angle this year. I was thinking how Christmas cards seem to be an outdated idea since we have Facebook and Twitter. But then again, I rarely use either, so maybe I am the one who is out of sync. I know that I enjoy hearing from each of my friends. I have been going through albums to create a family history in pictures for my granddaughters. Busily gathering pictures of great great grannies (who looked so serious about the whole deal—it was painful false teeth), I also came to the reality of the impact of family, ethical decisions, and roads less travelled.

Having become addicted to Ancestry.com, I have loved the discovery of these Revolutionary War grand daddies who also were described as God-fearing, or the establisher of a local church or often were ministers. As pioneers who eventually made their way to Texas, they did not become disillusioned or compromise their faith. That is a legacy that I hope to pass on. I thought every grandfather sat and sang hymns with his little granddaughter like mine did. I was surprised when I learned others didn't. Maybe that's why I didn't learn to be a good cook. I was busy singing.

And there is a song in our hearts this year. Derek, Melody & Skylar live outside Austin. Derek has created an App called GoVIP.

Apple has accepted it to go live soon. It has been seven years in the making, so he's hoping for a ring & jingle (in the family cash register—oops, another anachronism). Derek has invited me to go skiing with them as he takes Skylar (8th grade) for her first ski trip this December. She is now taller than me. I like to go skiing when I know I can still beat them down the slope. That is because she will be a beginner! I know that it won't be long before she will find the intermediate slopes that I like are boring.

Vance and Ashley are looking forward to the ring. . . of their front door. Last April their home caught fire in an electrical outlet in Evelyn's room, but fortunately most of the family were not at home. Only the family cat perished. Ashley and Vance know what it is to rebuild from ashes. I admire their fortitude and thankfulness. They should be back with a welcome mat in early Spring. I have enclosed a picture of my babysitting with their two girls (Mary Craddock and Evelyn) We were playing ballet. I encouraged the family dog (Carolina) to join in. That is one patient dog.

And my song must include Justin, of course. He has helped me with some investments. His song, naturally, is the Eyes of Texas (he's a little aggravated with them now even though he cheers with season tickets.) As for me, I returned to China in February in a subtle mission trip giving business seminars, then a summer mission trip to Tbilisi, Georgia. I'm going to Zambia, Africa in January working with the HIV orphans following Christmas. That would be the perfect time to get to see the massive wanderings of the wildlife in Tanzania's Serengeti. The vistas and time and effort make me realize how lucky I am.

That brings us back to our song of Christmas past and present. Mary, did you know your baby boy would give sight to the world as you kissed the face of God? As a mother, Mary remained in joyous trust. She saw and pondered these things in her heart. As a mother, a grandmother, and a friend, I remain in joyous trust. I wish the same for you and your family! Blessings, grace, peace & joyous trust!

From Eileen: Once again we were put in a holiday mood early this year with the arrival of eight or more inches of snow on October- Happy Birthday, Amelia! Since she started this ..."tradition of having a huge snowstorm in October" with her birth last year, we kind of expected an event- but this is getting scary! We managed to escape the wrath of Hurricane Sandy, although others down the coast weren't as fortunate. It might have something to do with the new insurance policy of a home generator!

We'll be celebrating Christmas early this year with a trip to Denver in mid-December. Can't wait to see the Colorado

Buchheits- especially since Amelia has started walking and talking! They came east in May for Amelia's Baptism- a lovely day! She wore her Great-great-grandfather's Christening gown and looked adorable! So nice to see Leslie's folks and hang out together- need to do that more often.

The Carneys of Bridgewater have a "big girl". Flynn is in kindergarten now and will be running the school in a year or two! We celebrated her fifth birthday at Disneyworld -what a joy to experience that magic through her eyes. Joe prepared for her to have a "Princess Birthday Luncheon". We were joined by all the Disney royalty, who stopped at the various tables for photo ops with the birthday girls. While the others were gushing about the beautiful dresses, etc., Flynn took Snow White aside to explain to her that you should never take fruit from a witch. Words of wisdom!

Meanwhile, the adult side of the clan has been keeping busy. Joe continues recruiting when he's not thinking up projects, visiting with the chicken girls, riding his tractor, helping shut-ins here in town and keeping up the maintenance on our Church- a full plate! I'm still fooling around with book signings and have started another book-this one for children- with an old friend who will do the illustrations. Another opportunity came up- to write a book with another Army buddy about the things we've learned from our children (joke here-it will be "short story"!)

Brigid continues her successes with United Health as a Programs Director. She travels a bit but manages to work from home most of the time- a neat trick since their house has been under repair and renovation for quite a while! Tim's been busy- and not only with the renovation. He's taken all the classes and state tests for certification as a fire fighter and EMT. Let's hope there's a place for him not too far from home! Horses continue to hold center stage for them both- except when Brigid is acting- her latest was the Novice in "Nunsense".

Brett and Leslie have been keeping the home fires burning- in yet another new house! They moved shortly after returning to Denver from the Christening. Leslie managed to find a place in their neighborhood -less than a block away! That girl was an Army wife in another lifetime! Brett does his commute to Littleton, managing to fit in walks with Amelia and Moose (who has adjusted nicely to having another creature in the house- especially one who drops food on the floor!).

We adopted a Black Lab named "Maynard" -their choice of name. All we could think of was "Dobie Gillis" -showing our age there. For those of you who remember our dog "Harry"- multiply the insanity by a factor of four and you're pretty close. Joe calls him "a work in progress"- riiiight. Come and visit and we'll be sure he's in the cage!

Let's Discuss

Eileen and I have had multiple songs this year from birthday to christening. The clanging sound of a firetruck to my son's home was a discordant note, that still has ramifications to this day—rebuilding from the ashes is certainly humbling. Thus, the songs have been happy and scary. But it brings us back to "Mary, did you know?" None of us can know what is in store.

1) Mary, did you know your baby boy would give sight to the world as you kissed the face of God? As a mother, Mary remained in joyous trust. She saw and pondered these things in her heart.
   What surprise turn did this last year take for you?

2) In Luke 1: 46-50, "And Mary said, 'My soul magnifies the Lord, and my spirit rejoices in God my Savior, for he has looked on the humble estate of his servant. For behold, from now on all generations will call me blessed: for he who is mighty has done great things for me and holy is his name. And his mercy is for those who fear him from generation to generation."
   Have you thought how you might pass down a Christmas tradition or Christian action from generation to generation?

Christmas Countdown, 2013

From Brenda:

One of the best parts of a Christmas letter is reaching out and touching friends who have always meant a great deal to me. Also, it forces me to retrospect. When I think of 2013, "stellar" comes to mind.

Then I realized "stellar" is why my year was so good. Wise men followed the star to gain a relationship with Christ. I've tried not to say "no" to opportunities this year in pursuit of that same star. Getting to Yes in a Land of No has brought some wonderful experiences. In January, I was in Zambia, Africa doing a Leadership Development seminar/camp with HIV orphaned girls ages 14-16. I then proceeded (alone) to Tanzania on a safari (which obviously looked a little strange since it was just me and the driver in open safari car.) In May, I taught a Management Behavior undergraduate course at LCC International University for a second time in Lithuania. In June I took Skylar (my 14 yr. old granddaughter) to St. Petersburg where I taught a two-week course at St. Petersburg Christian University. She hopped the metro subway in St. Petersburg with ease. We stopped in Paris in July. As we gazed at the Eiffel Tower, she informed me with a grin that she was moving to Paris. Finally, just today we had a pre-Thanksgiving lunch and all 3 sons plus 2 daughters-in-law and 3 granddaughters smiled for the camera out front of my soon to move from townhome.

Left to right:

Justin, Brenda, Vance, Mary Craddock & Evelyn, Melody, Ashley, Skylar & Derek & Athena the dog.

Eileen, Joe, Joe's Dad, Brigid, Leslie, Amelia, Brett and seated Flynn and Tim.

From Eileen's family on their porch, the smiling faces in the picture wish you a very happy holiday. We had a mini reunion this September and took advantage of it to take this shot. What a great group! We spent time with Amelia—oh, and her parents! We even had a pre-birthday party for her 2nd birthday. Lovely to have the whole clan together.

Our adventures in This Old House continue. This summer brought the joys of installing a new driveway. Oh, but FIRST, repair the stone walls next to it, replace the wooden fence which runs parallel to it, put in a different gate to the back yard, change the drainage system, level the whole enchilada and then wait for the appropriate weather to finish the remaining tasks. We started in June and finished in September. I must admit it looks great—and it's DONE. Have I mentioned done is my favorite word?

Joe has not changed hats but has added a few new ones. He continues to be very active in the not for profit he founded with a friend to help aging residents of the town remain, safely, in their own homes. "Community Caring in Bridgewater" has accomplished some really impressive things—an annual Health Fair, an energy audit and safety check, a shredding service for personal papers, a turn in service for medications, a "chores" service for minor home repairs, free fire extinguishers and smoke detectors—and the list goes on. He was asked to be the Veteran's Administration liaison for the town and has attended training sessions for that! Busy man!

Eileen has been asked to write another book by the competitor to her last one. She's working on getting access to the archives of a local museum to make that possible. Just to keep her busy, dear friend Brenda Shull wants to begin with her on a book which we hope will be both funny and spiritual. Eileen said she'd take care of the funny! This June, she hopes to join Brenda teaching in Albania with a stop in Poland for some ghostbusting and ancestor hunting!

The Carney clan is always on the move. Brigid's job with United Health has her in airports around the country. She rides her horse, Angelica, whenever possible and has picked up some ribbons for her efforts. Tim was selected by the New Haven Fire Department to join their ranks. He's waiting to hear the dates for training. Meanwhile, he's been chosen for the Planning and Zoning Commission in Bridgewater. Flynn has taken to gymnastics like a future Olympian. She fills in some free time with Hip Hop classes—if only they could bottle that energy!

The Denver Buchheits are kept busy keeping up with Amelia—that girl can go! Brett has been working on an alphabet book—his illustrations are a hoot and are bound to be a big hit with the parents reading to their kids. Oh, yes and he has his law practice! Leslie puts up with it all with grace. She was evacuated from her school in Aurora when the flood waters hit in the Fall. What a mess! Thankfully, they were spared any flooding.

As I watch fluffy flakes out my window, I'm thinking of a white Christmas, but whatever your weather, know that we are wishing you all the best for this Christmas season.

Let's Discuss:

Christmas is a time of family get togethers. But family isn't always about your blood relations. There are people who feel like family, whom you know you can count on, and maybe they are the ones you turn to for Christmas gatherings.

Let's face it. Families are like fudge, mostly sweet but there are a few nuts. Or a few who drive you nuts. One friend said the family photo made him smile because he was part of the family. He laughed because there was nothing that he could do about it.

I'm always wanting to take a family photo, but my adult children complain about the timing. It seems I want to take it just when the food has been served at the table and the food will get cold. Or just as everybody is trying to leave. So, I tested it and didn't mention it. Sure enough, no family photo that year. So, I remain my aggravating self and try to shoot candid shots.

Exodus 20:12 Honor your father and your mother, so that you may live long in the land the Lord, your God is giving you.

1) Are you prepared for the family gathering at Christmas to forgive some past actions on a family member's part? How much were your actions part of the problem?

2) Have you given thought to how you can avoid conflict with a particular family member this year by giving thought to their point of view ahead of time?

3) Can you apply 1 Corinthians 13:4-7 to your family gathering? Love is patient and kind; love does not envy or boast; it is not arrogant or rude. It does not insist on its own way; it is not irritable or resentful; it does not rejoice at wrongdoing but rejoices with the truth. Love bears all things, believes all things, hopes all things, endures all things. How would that work for you at your Christmas family gathering?

Christmas Countdown, 2014

From Brenda:

I will bet you remember your best gift ever. It was not the cost but the context—the giver who loved you and gave it to you that made it so special. Or you can remember some not-so-great gifts. I remember shortly after we married that David gave me a vacuum cleaner. Oops! We were newlyweds and did need a vacuum cleaner. Kindly, I had to disabuse him of practical gifts (that we would buy together for the house) as a birthday gift—I wanted the romantic context of something chosen just for me on my birthday or Christmas, large or small. Fortunately, he listened and did much better in later years.

This year has been a gift. Special blessings occurred like attending a Frosty puppet show and like making sugar cookies with Evelyn (4 yrs.) and Mary Craddock (6 yrs.) Creativity abounds. I never knew a Frosty cookie could look like that—with hair even.

Evelyn informed me that she had checked when she visited Santa and she was on "the good list." You learn a lot from grandkids. Mary Craddock informed me when kicking a soccer ball in the backyard with me and switching constantly so that whichever goal she kicked would now become her goal, that winning wasn't important. It was playing the game. Could she have heard that from Vance who was her YMCA soccer coach? Vance is also with her in Indian Princess and teaching teens in Sunday School with Ashley at their church. Ashley is also leading Mary Craddock's girl scout troop and the library at the pre-school. I asked Mary Craddock about her favorites at kindergarten. She is very social. She said her favorites are her teacher and the art classes, but what she *really* likes the most is helping her teacher teach. I'm sure the teacher appreciates Mary Craddock's expertise.

Derek and Melody are happy in Cedar Park, Texas attending half-time shows (the most important part of the high school football games) since Skylar is outstanding (unbiased) in Color guard. Skylar tosses flags and dances to complicated choreographed Texas award- winning routines. I attended one of her games. The band had instruments and electronic devices that did not even exist the last time I went to a high school game. Derek's auction company is excelling. To our delight, he is also a great "smoker" chef and upgraded our Thanksgiving smoked turkey to gourmet delicious. My dad (who is in a small residential care home) had Thanksgiving with us. At ninety he especially liked hugging the Shull girls. When asked if he slept well the night before, he answers, "I don't know, I was asleep." Or if asked how he is feeling, he answers, "Well, I'm here. The secret to a long life is waking up." His uncomplaining humor remains intact.

Justin returned from an exotic horseback trip into the wilds to hunt 4 legged beasts. We thought the bears would surrender, just seeing his outfitted gear. Unfortunately for him, the hunters only spotted a few 4 leggers so he didn't return with a trophy. I think the five days on horseback helped him decide that skiing & snowboarding are looking good for a winter sport. Hunting on horseback, not so much. (Score one for the bears).

I have been asked to light the advent candle next Sunday. I think about Mary's journey to Bethlehem and how the journey took her to places out of her comfort zone. She had anticipation and hope. I hosted two Nigerians and went on two mission trips this year teaching undergraduate Management courses in June in Lehza, Albania with side trips to Monte Negro and Greece. In November it was three weeks in Tbilisi, Georgia, and Amsterdam. The blessing is mine on these trips. (The blessing is that someone listens to me & acts like I know what I am talking about ☺) It all goes back to that advent candle and the best gift ever. The best gift was not only the cost but the context—a gift specifically chosen for me and for you. How blessed we are to be the chosen children of God.

From Eileen.

Here is a riddle—what do the Great Pyramid and our new laundry room have in common? The time it took to finish! We started construction on an addition off the kitchen of our 1848 Connecticut farmhouse in August. We are just getting the finishing touches for Christmas. The end product gives us both pantry and laundry areas plus a large sewing/craft space for Eileen and an elevator to bring heavy items—and people—from the garage into the kitchen wing. It is well worth the wait.

Obviously, it has been a busy year for the Buchheits. For Joe, it meant acting as the general contractor for this construction while continuing his work for CCB (Community Caring in Bridgewater). This volunteer organization helps senior citizens who are living alone. They do great work! Joe also marches on in his help at our Church doing everything from overseeing paving in the parking lot to lock replacement. Multiple hats and multiple talents! That guy is getting stars in his crown!

2014 was the year to fulfill a long-awaited wish for Eileen to visit her grandfather's ancestral town in Poland. It was an amazing trip, and she is writing a book about it. Just by chance, she bumped into an acquaintance here in town, Leonard Bernstein's baby brother, Burt. He spent a lifetime at the "New Yorker" and is an author of 12 books. He offered to mentor her through this book. What a gift!

The Carneys have been busy, too. Brigid went to work for Affinity Health Plan as VP/Corporate Quality and Performance last spring. She has been applying LEAN practices to their systems. The commute is a killer, but the title looks lovely. Her husband, Tim, fulfilled his life-long desire to become a firefighter. He graduated last month and is working in New Haven. And last, but not least is Flynn, now 7. She is quite an athlete—swimming, gymnastics, and horse-back riding with a hip-hop class after school for good measure.

Our Denver Buchheits have been thriving, too. The whole clan made the trip east in August. Brett got commandeered to hawk raffle tickets at the Bridgewater Fair. He earned a permanent invitation to come back anytime. Millie and Leslie hung out at the farm while the menfolk went fly fishing on the Housatonic River. Leslie is working as a teacher in Aurora and Millie goes to Goddard School's 3-year-old class. Her finger painting won a ribbon at the Bridgewater Fair. In the meantime, Brett returned earlier this month to help us celebrate Joe's dad 90th birthday. The celebrants got to wear t-shirts emblazoned with Dad's picture in full fire fighter's regalia. I do not know who had more fun—the celebrants or Dad.

Let's Talk:

We have brought up the "Best Gift Ever" idea. This coincides with James 1:17:

Every good gift and every perfect gift are from above, coming down from the Father of lights with whom there is no variation or shadow due to change.

1) What is the best non-material gift you have received?

2) Yesterday is history, tomorrow is a mystery, today is a gift, that is why we call it the present. What present can you give someone else today?

3) Is your presence a present for someone? Are you a resource or a roadblock?

Christmas Countdown, 2015

From Brenda:

Do you remember the childhood "Star light, star bright, first star I see tonight? I wish I may, I wish I might, have this wish I wish tonight?" Well, I admit I still do it. Last night while walking in the crisp, cool and clear air, I was struck by the fact that it was a star that led us to the best wish fulfillment of all. Christ still leads and helps us to a relationship with God. Out of darkness came light.

2015 has brought some wonderful wishes. One of the best is that Vance and Ashley were surprised to learn that they will have a 3rd miracle baby in 2016. Mary Craddock (7 yrs.) and Evelyn (5 yrs.) will be big sisters to a little brother. And they are naming him: David! We learned this amazing fact the week before Vance's family, and I traveled to Disneyworld. (It was a wish that had a full year of planning to go to Disneyworld).

My grandchildren call me Gram. While we were at Disneyworld, Evelyn asked me if I knew where Gram World was. I asked, "Where? "She said in a sweet small voice, "In my heart." Wow.

With melting knees, I thought that this kid is getting to go back to Disneyworld when little David is big enough.

It is a wish come true for Derek who has had a huge year with his Austin auction business and was named in the top Texas auctioneers. His wife Melody has joined his business. Another blessing come true is their daughter. Skylar turned 16, was voted Captain in Color Guard as well as Honor Society. We cannot believe in all fairness that Derek has such a golden child who would not even consider a piercing or tattoo. Or at least she is not telling.

Justin is pursuing a lifelong plan of starting his own real estate investment business. It is incubating. Possibilities are that 2016 will bring a wedding, but he is not telling. He is a chip off the block. I had to buy my wedding dress on sale in December before David popped the question to me in January for a potential June wedding. He delayed. I forged ahead. A girl must plan!! So, perhaps wedding bells next summer for Justin.

Have you ever wished in July that you could escape to Alaska? For the month of July, I was with Alaska Missions in Kenai, helping during the salmon frenzy for the locals. We may have been sleeping on cots, but 66 degrees was a huge contrast to Dallas 100+ heat.

This year also brought me a little black fur—dog style. A friend offered a Havanese female puppy. One look into those brown eyes and I had to go to dog training school so I could learn potty training again. Her name is Raphaella, but she is Raffi to her friends. If you meet her, you are a friend. I did not know I was wishing for a dog, but she did.

I also started "flipping" houses—renovating to sell. I was watching HGTV and figured I could do that too! I did one in March, another in August and the one in October is still in progress, but good so far. At this point, the market is good. Basically, it is an excuse to shop. It may be tile, counter tops, faucets, wood floors, etc. but it is shopping. I have found excellent crews. I know this is one of the secrets to success. Who said you cannot be your own general contractor?

A bittersweet note is that my dad died just after Valentines. But at 90.5, he was ready to join his Sweetheart. My mother had died fifteen years earlier. I still miss him, but it was God's timing and no suffering.

I am counting my blessings in wish fulfillment and hoping that you are happy, healthy and surrounded in Starlight/Sonlight. May your 2016 be filled with light out of darkness.

From Eileen: 2015 was a year of beginnings and endings for us, as well. Joe's dad, or as we called him "G.G" for great grandfather passed away in June. Because it was his desire to be buried in Arlington with Mom, we couldn't have his final service until mid-November. A challenging time.

But, as is so often the case, while that sadness was evolving, other happier events were taking place. High on the list was the news of another Buchheit coming into our lives—Brett, Leslie and Millie will be welcoming a new sister/daughter in February. Her name will be "Josephine." That would have tickled G.G. Meanwhile, Brett has decided his days of sports cars are behind him...for now—and he is getting a more "parental" vehicle.

Other happy news items included the publication of, not one but two books by Buchheit ladies. Brigid wrote "The Jake House." It's a children's story telling the tale of an Irish immigrant family of firefighters at the turn of the 19th century. It will be the first in a series. J.K. Rowling, watch out! You can see the fun website if you go online.

Eileen also published a book, this time in the form of a Kindle on Amazon.com books. The title is "You must call him Joseph." It's a memoir telling of her twenty-five-year long search for her grandfather's ancestors in Poland. Her next effort will require a trip to Germany to search for maternal ancestors. Do you see a theme here?

Joe continues to be active in golf and his not-for-profit organization providing services for seniors here in Bridgewater. He is the V.A. point of contact for the town as well and is the "go to" guy for all things at our church. What is retirement?

Tim continues putting out fires and saving folks in New Haven—his lifelong dream. This summer he helped on our "To do List," making this old house a happier and healthier place. He and Flynn took regular swims in the pool, with Flynn now doing gymnastic dives off the board.

We all gathered for the Bridgewater Country Fair in August. For such a tiny town, it's hard to believe that thousands of folks make us their destination every year. It is a window into the past, seeing shearing of sheep, tractor parades, pig races and countless other events. It really is something out of Norman Rockwell. Flynn and Millie had the chance to hang out together as cousins. Both girls show signs of artistic genes—again, thanks G.G.! Meanwhile, Leslie proved to be an expert in logistics and had arranged a move to a larger home to be timed for their return to Denver. Go girl!!

Let's Discuss

Star light, star bright! Thank you, God for the ability to wish upon a star and find the light that you provide in a happy, hopeful ' something better push back.' Albert Camus, a French philosopher and journalist said, "In the midst of winter, I found there was, within me, an invincible summer. And that makes me happy. For it says that no matter how hard the world pushes against me, within me, there is something stronger—something better, pushing right back."

1) Have you thought about this quote? What action would you take if it were guaranteed that you could not fail to make this Christmas something better, something stronger?

2) Have you found amid winter, there was something within, pushing back with hope?

3) The Magi could not have had a smooth trip. Travel was difficult and dangerous. However, they had resources to fall back on. They had a star guiding them. They got to Jerusalem and the scribes helped them to locate Bethlehem. This is what the Church is meant to be—people and resources that help us on the journey to the Lord. Have you made use of these resources at Christmas?

Christmas Countdown, 2016

From Brenda:

A Chinese proverb says, "That the birds of worry and care fly above your head, this you cannot change. But that they build nests in your hair, this you can prevent." It is that time of year where bad hair days are a little more frequent. The good news is that I don't have to worry about cooking. Clever, ornately prepared food is not appreciated—it makes my granddaughters reject it for Chick fil A and my sons have always regarded it suspiciously. After all, a perfectly managed meal, correct in every detail, is a sure sign of someone who doesn't have enough to do—or they really, really enjoy cooking for others who are delighted with their cuisine. Neither describes me.

What I love about Christmas is that we are amped up on sugar, Hallmark tv shows, Christmas bell ringing in the mall, candlelit musical church services and Hope. God went silent for 400 years between the Old Testament and the New. Sometimes His silence allows Time to beat down the dreams in our heart. But then a year like 2016 shows me that God does not want the ordinary in our dreams, marriage, or work. God loves showing us the impossible. So here is 2016.

First "impossibility": Ashley and Vance welcomed their baby boy born early in April rather than May. And they named him David. This baby "surprised" them. There were no required fertility drugs. It also took one month of Ashley being bedridden in the hospital to keep him from coming too soon, but she did it! It is my first grandson, very relaxed and easy, as he joins his two bigger sisters Evelyn (Kindergarten) and Mary Craddock (Second Grade). One lesson learned is God's timing. Then Evelyn taught us another. She wanted to be Mary in the Kindergarten play but was selected as a camel. So, the first Wise Man stepped forward and said, "I brought Gold." The second, "I brought Myrrh;" the Third said, "I brought frankincense." Evelyn stepped forward in her cute camel costume and said, "I brought **them**." She got resounding applause and laughter. So, even if you are a camel, you're important. How else would the Wise Men have made it in time?

Next "Impossibility" was long awaited: Justin was wearing nonstop smiles. He said he smiled so much that his cheeks got sore as he beamed for two days straight. He and Raven had a beautiful destination wedding in Beaver Creek, Colorado surrounded by old friends and family. It only took Justin five years to pop the question, but this is a marriage made in Heaven. Just after the ceremony started, the Aspen leaves started to quake in a refreshing soft breeze lasting a full two minutes. The minister remarked it was a gift from heaven. It made me smile because I knew that David had just turbojetted in from Heaven. I do not think David missed his son's ceremony and the quaking breeze proved it. I know he was there in our hearts.

Third "impossibility" is that Derek's Auction business has doubled and sometimes tripled this year beyond his dreams. My entrepreneurial son is on a roll. Skylar is turning 18. She is a senior in high school deciding on which university is right for her and vice versa that they select her.

Finally, the "possible" is that I will be touring New Zealand/Australia in January. This crosses off a big one on my bucket list

So now we hear from Eileen:

Winter came early to Connecticut this year. Good friend, Brenda Shull, was visiting from Dallas when the first snow fell- in October! Her stay here was both business and pleasure. She and Eileen are putting the finishing touches on the book they've been writing together for the past few years. It will take a while before you see it in the stores!

The high point in 2016 was the birth of Josephine Grace Buchheit in February- such a sweetie! We managed a trip to Denver to introduce ourselves and it was love at first sight! Millie is an excellent Big Sister and is enjoying the role. She and her Daddy left Mom and JoJo at home in August to fly east for the Bridgewater Fair. Leslie quite rightly said that she would need a bit more time before she'd be ready for the Fair! While the adults (less Eileen) were off playing golf, the younger set (with Eileen) was hanging out at the farm. We were joined by Cousin Luke Strang for all the activities, including ceramics. They all made coffee mugs- very creative crowd! Then, we were off to the Fair where both Flynn and Nonna won red ribbons for their ceramic pieces. When we explained that "red" meant second place, Luke said, "You were robbed." Gotta love that kid!

This has been a rough year health wise for Eileen. She had pneumonia twice, once requiring a stay in the hospital. We had thought a trip to Barbados would be the thing to bump up her

immune system. Now, she insists a follow up trip to Disney with all the family is the true cure!

There isn't a busier guy in Bridgewater than Joe. He is still the point of contact from the VA to local veterans. That also requires regular articles for the town's newsletter. He continues to be active with CCB (Community Caring in Bridgewater) and has "regulars" -ladies of a certain age who need some help to stay happy and healthy in their own homes. As I write this, he is off to the annual retreat in Hartford for the weekend with other men from our parish. Then, there are the critters on the farm that call to him when he goes out the door! Golf fills in whatever time is left free- even if he must move some other stuff around to make that happen!

Tim recently celebrated his second anniversary as a Firefighter. He still loves his work- great fit! Brigid and he were on TV this fall. A New Haven firehouse was slated for downsizing, and they spoke about the importance it has in the neighborhood. Brigid spoke about her book, "The Jake House", and donated copies to folks who would visit the house and sign a petition. It is still open, so it must be working! In their free time, they have taken to golf with a vengeance. Flynn is a golfer, too, having participated in her first tourney this summer- and winning!

That brings us full circle for another year.

Let's Discuss:

1) Have you ever had a Christmas that was impossible, but it all became possible?

Eileen tells about her mother. Her mother was talented, but not in cooking. She was bereft when she was preparing the stuffing for the Christmas turkey and the egg she cracked into the breading mixture was rotten. The whole kitchen was enveloped in the rotten smell! But, in its own way it was a blessing, said Eileen. Because my mother's stuffing was awful, having the empty turkey was a vast improvement (that we were secretly thankful for!). An impossible meal became savory.

2) Have you been chosen a camel when you wanted to be Mary? How did that turn out?

Eileen's granddaughter was selected to be Mary and was chagrined that she had no speaking part. So, Flynn enhanced the non-speaking part. With great flourish she folded her hands in prayer and bowed her head. Then she genuflected which was unusual for a Congregational church. The audience loved it. Brigid said her Catholic background would "out." Flynn gave it her all.

Fairview Farm

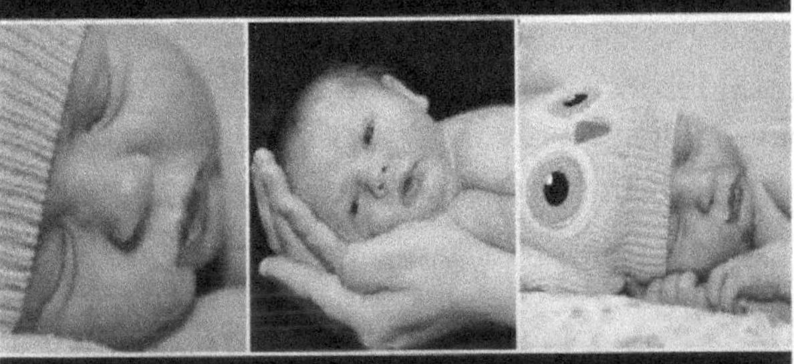

JCB

Josephine Grace Buchheit

February 21, 2016 – 8 pounds 2 ounces – 19.5 inches

Christmas Countdown, 2017

From Brenda:

It is the happiest time of the year! So here I am in a new address. I moved back a few blocks to the same gated community that I lived in earlier. My dog and I really missed the green space. This house has walks, plus geese & ducks & still is just minutes away from grandkids. It is also close to the largest mall in Dallas. The one where you find traffic jams even though you have not gotten out of the parking lot.

Speaking of seasonal wandering, my friend Kay Custis mentioned that if the Wise Men had been Wise Women, they would have asked for directions and arrived on time, shopped for practical gifts, helped deliver the baby, cleaned up the place and made casseroles. The last is doubtful because most of my women friends have given up baking casseroles. But, cooking never was my forte.

So how has 2017 treated you? For the Shull families, Raven and Justin enjoyed celebrating their first year of marriage. They celebrated milestone birthdays with trips to Costa Rica, and helping friends celebrate milestone birthdays in exotic travel. They enjoyed a long-planned trip to Italy. It's Dr Seuss land with so much to see and so little time!

Vance and Ashley have experienced the wonder of baby David growing into toddlerhood this year. He is walking and finds that whatever his two sisters are doing is much more fun than playing with his toys. He skipped over saying "Mama". His first words are "Football" and with great zest, he throws both arms in the air indicating a touchdown. Evelyn, in first grade, told me she probably has outgrown the Disney store toys. With this, she skillfully tossed her scarf over her shoulder and informed me that **she** is a fashionista. When I asked her which room of my new house she wanted, she said the one with the balcony, so she could set up her art easel and paint. (She has great imagination. This is a to-be-discovered talent. I do not know that she has ever picked up a serious paint brush). Mary Craddock excelled with her first month-long camp experience (a milestone of being away from home) at her mom's alumnae Camp Mystic. M.C. received best camping awards and is looking forward to going back. I saw growth and happiness in her.

But we also had a miracle in Derek's family. Due to quick action on Melody's part, doctors and I believe help from the Lord, Derek's brain stem stroke in the Spring did not result in permanent paralysis. He has recovered beautifully with few side effects. This Fall, Skylar entered U.T. San Antonio, so Derek and Melody are trudging through the empty nest syndrome. To their credit, they have traveled together and bonded well. They both are enjoying the building success of Derek's company being named one of Texas best at ATXAuctions.com. He barely missed a few weeks of work after total right-side paralysis with the stroke.

So how about me? Please tell Santa I have been good***ish.***

I have realized there are 4 stages of life. 1) You believe in Santa Claus, 2) You do not believe in S.C., 3) You ***are*** S.C. and 4) You look like Santa Claus. I think I know what I got for Christmas—5 pounds. It started with getting to go to New Zealand and Australia, then traveling with women friends to Colorado where we did zip line, biking & hiking, but also tasting the grape and eating dessert first. A season of gladness, a season of cheer and to top it off, a wonderful year! My prayer is the same for you!!! May God bless you all!!

From Eileen: Our holiday greetings come a bit early this year as we are leaving shortly to celebrate—in Bermuda! Why this location? Brigid has, once again, found an amazing opportunity. This time she is a vice president for the Argus Group, using her background in Lean and logistics to streamline their systems. Eventually, she will cover other islands as well. Their very British style is a direct contrast to our high energy daughter, who has earned the nick name of "The Energizer Bunny."

Flynn has become a Bermuda girl and enjoys snorkeling after school—off their private beach! She's attending the Warwick Academy, a 350-year-old school which boasts multiple Rhodes scholars. Her pronunciation is slowly becoming British. She's in a "form" not a "class" or "grade." Graduates of this school have an automatic invitation to Oxford. Wow!

Tim continues his work in firefighting, serving the city of New Haven. He has worked out a schedule so he can work two weeks on and be in Bermuda the next ten days. Millennial families certainly look different these days! In between, he is getting their New Milford property ready for sale. His hope is to find an efficiency apartment in New Haven to shorten his commute. We should all have his energy!

The Denver Buchheits are busy also. Brett has moved his law offices to a new location and is expanding his practice. In his down time, he has become a woodworker—birdhouses are his specialty, and his artistic consultant is Millie, now a kindergarten student and very much a BIG sister to JoJo. We had a special visit with the clan in October and were amazed at how fast they are growing! JoJo is a delight, making faces is her specialty. Leslie manages to keep them on track and at the same time is teaching a first-grade class in nearby Aurora. She loved teaching kindergarten and misses it but has a few of her students from last year.

Joe continues his activities—golf, volunteering with Community Caring in Bridgewater, golf, working at Church, golf, keeping this house and farm going—did I mention GOLF? He also has checked out a beautiful course in Bermuda. Do you see a trend there?

I am still working on my new journal, this one on my German ancestors. Finding an Oldenburg genealogist has proven to be a challenge. I'll be making my way to Deutschland soon. I'm in the running for Town Historian –I'll let you know how that works out!

Let's Discuss:

1) Both the Shulls and the Buchheits experienced a great deal of hope this year. Emily Dickinson wrote that "hope is the thing with feathers, that perches in the soul and sings the tune without the words, and never stops at all." Hope is persistent, even when darkness closes in. Like a bird that cannot be silenced, hope persists despite all odds. How can hope renew your strength this Christmas season?

2) The Advent wreath is a Christian tradition derived from a secular practice. During the dark days of December, people used to light candles on wreaths as a sign of hope for the light to come with spring. During the Middle Ages, the wreath was adapted to prepare for Christmas with Christ as light of the world. What is the difference between optimism and hope? How are these different concepts to you?

3) "O Little Town of Bethlehem" is a popular Christmas hymn written in the 19th century by Phillips Brooks. He wrote the hymn after riding horseback from Jerusalem to

Bethlehem on Christmas Eve. The third stanza was never included in publication. Here it is:

O Little town of Bethlehem
Where Children pure and happy
Pray to the blessed Child,
Where misery cries out to thee,
Son of the undefiled.
Where charity stands watching
And faith holds wide the door,
The dark night wakes, the glory breaks,
And Christmas comes once more.

Where do you see faith holding wide the door?

Christmas Countdown, 2018

From Eileen:

Christmas this year brings us to the brink of a very special occasion. On January 4th*, 2019, will mark our 50*th *anniversary. We've been celebrating since last spring, starting with a family trip to Disneyland—great fun to be with Millie and JoJo in a magical place! Flynn missed out, as her "school trip" took her from Bermuda to Washington, D.C.—better luck next time! She has had an amazing experience at the Warwick Academy in Bermuda—with electives like golf, scuba and cricket!*

Brigid was selected to give a presentation in Berlin in May. This was a perfect opportunity for me to go to Germany. I hadn't been back since long before the Wall came down. It was an amazing experience to be in a hotel in the east overlooking so much of what had been closed off the last time I was there. Finding a piece of the wall took some effort. The government has declared it a crime to remove pieces of the wall. So many people had been helping themselves to small rocks that the German government was worried it would disappear completely. The police call these souvenir snatchers "woodpeckers."

To continue our future anniversary celebration, we cruised to Bermuda in October. There were singing waiters and wine delivered to our suite. Then we jumped ship to go to Brigid's house until the end of the month. Since Brigid and Flynn will be returning to the States this month, it was bittersweet to know it was our last time in Southampton. Who knows where Brigid's next job will take her? Tim is looking forward to having his girls under the same roof for a while! They will stay in his New Haven apartment until a final decision is made.

Brett and Leslie are welcoming an unusual pet in their family—one fit for royalty—a falcon. Millie and JoJo will share in the adventure. (It's never dull in this family.) Millie has begun her elementary school experience in a program for Gifted and Talented. JoJo is still at the Goddard school for preschoolers.

Joe continues volunteering at Church and in town. He's busy but not so busy that he could turn down two rescue donkeys. Their names will be bestowed by Flynn. She said you can't name an animal until you meet face to face. We also adopted two barn cats to combat the unwelcome visitors with four little feet and long skinny tails. What I didn't know is that they like to bestow "presents" of their hunting triumphs. I must step carefully when I go out to the ceramic kiln. You never know where a "gift" /body will be placed. I never saw that in the Tom and Jerry cartoons. But then, Tom never caught Jerry!

I've been enjoying my new position as Town Historian. I write articles for the newsletter and do research for folks trying to find out more about their families or homes in the area. I am still planning a trip to Oldenburg on another European adventure to find out more about my own ancestors of long ago.

And from Brenda: Why is it so cold at Christmas in 2018? Because it's Decembrrrrrr!!

This year in 2018 Jackson Alexander Shull was born. He is my fifth grandchild and Justin and Raven's first born. They were so gracious (and excited) to include me in his pre- natal wonder, like viewing the first sonogram and getting updates on his womb growth (the size of a pecan, then avocado, etc.) He weighed in at 7lbs. 9 oz. and was in the 85% of height so I knew if a fight broke out in the nursery, he'd be ok!

Since it is the Christmas season, I thought about God's planning for the birth of His own Son. It was in Bethlehem, which seemed like an inconvenient donkey ride. But that was the birthplace of King David, and it was foretold centuries before that it would be Bethlehem. His birth was visited by the rich and the poor. The amazing visit of the Wise Men with their gifts of gold, etc. provided income for Mary and Joseph for the next few years in their escape to Egypt. The unwashed shepherds provided that human touch and promise that Jesus was available for all. The next few years, Jesus studied and learned, growing in wisdom and stature. It gave Him time to fully understand His identity. Then, when he was baptized, and at his pinnacle, He entered the Wilderness. Isn't that just like us? Just when we think we have success and starting to "get it," we enter the wilderness of challenging times where we learn a lot more. When he came out of the wilderness, he called his disciples. We too need to establish a community of friends to make our life richer. We cannot do without friends and community. Finally, He was on his way to fulfill His purpose. And we, too, go on our way with purpose driven lives.

This year I found new learning experiences of purpose. I was in Costa Rica with Highland Park Methodist church where we worked with orphaned and abused children. Even though I had been with orphaned children before in Africa & Guatemala, it reminded me that traumatized children really need hugs, laps and patient playfulness in safety. In July I was with Delta Gamma in Toronto at the Canadian Institute for the Blind working with children with limited vision. These were brave little hearts surrounded by darkness who trusted us to leap off and onto the subway, carousel rides, and paddle boats in the bay. Fearful, but trusting, they faced challenges that gave me greater appreciation for my sight. Then, in the Fall, I went to Cuba which gave me greater appreciation for my freedom. I talked to a doctor who complained of the lack of antibiotics and having to re-use syringes and re-use plastic gloves in the hospital. Repressed wages and limited opportunities were nothing like my life in the States.

And, in the meantime, I experience the joy of grand mothering. Skylar is in her second successful year at U.T., San Antonio. In contrast, Baby Jackson is starting his baby smiles. He has an early toothy grin that captures your heart. Mary Craddock is captain of her soccer team in the fourth grade. Evelyn is successfully conquering the second grade taking drama classes mixed with soccer which Vance is coaching. David is a happy, relaxed two-year-old where his mother is president of his pre-school. With three kids, she is not so relaxed!!!

We are all working on God's timing and development. When it comes down to it, hard times or good, we are blessed!

Let's Discuss:

1) There is a story which tells of a king who announced a competition "To all artists in the land, bring me your best depiction of peace. Whoever can best depict the concept of peace will be granted the title of chief painter." The artists sent in their finest work. One frontrunner depicted a glassy lake perfectly mirroring snowcapped mountains in serene settings. However, when the curtain covering the winning painting was dropped, everyone was shocked. This winner also depicted a mountain, but it had a stormy sky filled with lightning in brash strong strokes. As the onlookers gazed closer, they slowly noticed a small bush tucked into a crack on the side of the mountain. Inside the bush was a mother bird on her nest, sitting quietly—at

perfect peace. How can we tap into sustaining peace the next time a storm develops?

2) Have you felt like that mother bird in the crush of Christmas? What are some ways that you personally gather peace in this busy-ness? A walk-outdoors in nature, a scheduled meditation time? What in your busy life can be altered to allow more opportunities to see, hear and hold more peace?

3) Psalm 119 says “Your word is a lamp to my feet and a light to my path.” God illuminates just enough of our walk for us to take the next step. Have you asked for direction to your purpose, knowing that the wilderness will be there, and a community of friends will help? Has this year (as for Brenda and Eileen) brought new learning experiences of purpose?

Christmas Countdown, 2019

From Eileen: Is it Christmas, AGAIN???

We have had a strange year. . .even for us! I had a bad fall in February. The doctor at the hospital asked if the damage was from skiing or if I had been run over by a truck. In fact, . . .I slipped on the ice on our back porch and fractured both knees and tore both ACLs and MCLs. It was so easy to do on that snow covered porch! I have spent the remainder of 2019 in recovery, getting my legs back together again. From wheelchair, to walker, to slowly gaining my speed, it was truly a humbling and learning experience. let us hope 2020 sees me moving more and for sure hurting less.

Joe's dream of making a farm animal rescue from part of the farm acreage has come true. For years he's been taking in the dysfunctional and geriatric. Now he is "official"—right down to the website, Fairvufarm.org, a 501 (c) 3. Next year we'll send pictures of the gang with the addition of 2 donkeys, Mrs. Pickles and Boomerang. He is still active in the Community Caring group and little old ladies call on a regular basis. As a little old lady, myself, I can fully understand that! Add to the list activities from Church and he has at least two full time jobs in retirement—besides golf.

Our three granddaughters are growing like weeds, each developing their own personality and talents. What a pleasure to see them develop! Millie is in a Gifted Program in Denver and is a budding actress. JoJo is in the Goddard School Program and loves books. Flynn is excelling in her new school, Hamden Hall, and has made new friends there after leaving Bermuda. She has even been invited to spend a vacation in China with a new friend. Brett and Leslie are still holding down the fort in Colorado and loving it. Their weather would make a challenge for anyone to dress in—blizzard one day and shorts the next. Brett's new offices have worked out well and Leslie is still teaching in Aurora. They keep going with swim lessons, plays and project.

Our biggest Christmas gift last year was Brigid and Flynn returning to the States following the conclusion of Brigid's contract in Bermuda. That gave her the chance to complete her master's and get her applications ready for a PhD. She and Tim are looking for a new house in the New Haven area. Tim is still the happiest firefighter in New Haven. He's running for office in his Union this year. If only you all could vote!!

We will be thinking of past holidays and remembering times well spent. If visiting, remember to bring carrots—LOTS of carrots!!

From Brenda:
Holly Jolly Greetings for Christmas of 2019!

Have you noticed how early people started decorating for Christmas this year? Since Raven and Justin were hosting our family's Thanksgiving Dinner at their new home, I put my energy into decorating early for Christmas. I think the lights on the pumpkins looked kinda good.

It has been said that "He who has not Christmas in his heart will never find it under the tree." Feeling exhausted from decorating, I thought about stretching out under the tree in hopes my family would see me as a gift. Somehow, I do not know if passers-by in the darkest of the night will truly appreciate my teetering on the ladder to hang a garland of lights around my porch and hedges. But there go the Griswolds and me! Candle watts galore!

Research says there is a link between thankful people and happy people. If you are content in the Now—it is amazing what the Now becomes! And this is one happy, grateful chick! Sometimes it is hard to see the Masterpiece in Christmas because we are busy looking at the mess. I read that in the Olympics, Bronze medal winners are happier than Silver Medal winners. The Silver Medalist is focused on the fact they missed the Gold by tiny fractions. The Bronze Medalist is simply happy to have made it to the stage. Gratitude perpetuates the notes of joy. So, it is with a joyful heart that I am reporting on my stage:

Derek's business of ATX Auctions (online) is now expanding and they are opening an Exercise Outlet in Utah. My granddaughter Skylar is still happily majoring in Communications at UT San Antonio.

Justin and Raven are watching 14-month-old Jackson who is not just walking but running. They are amazed daily at his development from a newborn last year to a happy, talking, thinking, smiling toddler. I love seeing the happiness and joy that they have in being parents. They have just found out that baby number two will arrive in August.

Meanwhile, Vance and Ashley are proud of their three: Mary Craddock is doing very well in the transition to middle school 5th grade. Evelyn has been chosen for select competition in Atlanta in hip hop dance and she loves her drama classes. She has a very fertile imagination. And while I was at Grand Parents Day, the Pre-School teacher rushed over to tell me how David was the kindest 3-year-old she had ever met. Honest. I am not making that up! Shades of Grandpa David. (Of course, I give credit to Ashley & Vance, but it was déjà vu.)

Gratitude rips the rear-view mirror off our past. It keeps us moving forward.

Let's Discuss:

Eileen spent the last year in 2019 in recovery from an accidental fall on some slippery snowy ice. She did not choose this disaster, nor did it happen because she was negligent. She evolved from wheelchair to walker to finally walking again. Even in our darkest moments, or moments of great joy or thanksgiving, God cares for us, and He is with us. And because God is with us, ***the storms around us do not have to become storms within us.*** Let us read Psalms 23 (The Lord is my Shepherd . . .) and discuss!

1. What did this Psalm make you feel? What thoughts or images came to mind as you read it?

2. What does this Psalm reveal about us as people?

3. What does this Psalm reveal about God?

4. How can you begin to pray this Psalm today over yourself? What about those around you?

Christmas Countdown, 2020

Merry Christ-masked from my bubble to yours!

Craziness has been a constant companion as I bought 60 gallons of bottled water and played tug of war over 48 rolls of toilet paper. Any venture out into the strangely deserted streets brought spritzes of Lysol from head to foot when I returned. My Online Dance/Exercise classes dwindled from four to none weekly. Going to the grocery store became a scarce but strategically planned adventure. Carefully peering down the aisle, I tried to outrun any buggies and avoid any incoming unsuspecting shoppers going the wrong way. And Christmas shopping has been online which is tough on the inveterate shopper like me who likes to examine and imagine the merchandise. I always thought going to the mall of your choice was a Christmas must-do.

I was thinking about which verse for Covid Christmas 2020 would be appropriate and Matthew 1:23 seemed the obvious choice: Behold, a virgin shall be with child, and shall bring forth a son, and they shall call his name **Emmanuel**, which is, **God with us**.

This unusual year has meant we needed God with Us in a real and personal way. Fear is a constant companion that pops up and holds us down.

Even in the best of times, we fear losing our job; but then, after a while, we fear getting stuck and keeping that job!

We become afraid when change is in the air. Then we become afraid that there will be no change and we are stuck in a rut.

We stop in the darkness just short of victory. But God nudges us forward each step of our journey.

For Raven and Justin, it has brought working from home, so I needed to help with Jackson, now two years old. He is a child in constant outdoor play, running with gusto, suddenly stopping, and giving me a knee hug, and then returning to whatever make believe sport he is playing—football, basketball, and yes, golf is his favorite. It is his version, but amazing for a child so young. In August, God delivered his baby sister, Olivia Wren, safely. She is a beautiful baby girl who dissolves in a smile and melts the viewer. She is patient and a calm baby.

Derek and Melody have had their best year ever with ATXAuctions, an online auction business that has locations now in Utah, California and across Texas. Skylar is a Senior, set to graduate from U.T., San Antonio in May 2021 in Communications. Covid has not held her back!

Vance has made Partner and worked from home and office. Ashley has successfully survived remote learning for Evelyn, now 10 and Mary Craddock, 12. Evelyn has continued in her dream to stay in dance & drama and Mary Craddock was selected Best Camper or Cup Girl Junior division at Camp Mystic. David at 4 yrs. is into dinosaurs and Bat Man. He is not a big talker. At the dinner table, this boy- of- few- words surprised his family, by sighing and saying, "Life is so complicated."

And so it goes. My hope is that you and yours are safe, healthy, and happy. Our family gatherings have been sparse and socially distanced. Living alone is not my cup of tea, but I have been blessed with a walking trail in my gated community and Raffi who will sit by the door in case I forget to take her out for a walk. at least three times a day. Emmanuel is born, **God is with us** and for that we are Blessed! Cyber hugs!

Merry Christmas from Eileen:

It does seem odd to say "Merry" when we think about all the terrible things of 2020. I'm trying hard to concentrate on the good – here goes.

I am smiling when I think of Halloween. Not that we had any Trick or Treaters, but because our granddaughter, JoJo, announced that her costume would be "Doctor Princess" – and so she was! She had her favorite Princess Elsa dress topped with a white shirt – worked for her! Her sister, Millie, has become the Queen of Legos – we see a future in architecture for her! Such imagination! Their parents are working from home. God knows how long this insanity will last. We wish them well -and hope they stay healthy.

Brigid, Tim and Flynn are enjoying their "New/Old" house in Woodbridge. They promised themselves that they wouldn't start any major indoor projects for the first year. That left them open to gardening and fencing the whole place – some 4 acres. Brigid found that she had my grandmother's green thumb and is well on her way to becoming a Master Gardener. In the meantime, Brigid's horse, Sir Ian, came back from his hiatus in upstate New York. He had his longtime friend, Cooper, come along for company. Cooper is older than dirt. That meant more fence and a LOT more feed – he's an eater! Flynn has the role of "Puck" in "Midsummer's Night's Dream" and is loving it. Tim has been exposed to Covid on two occasions and was quarantined both times but tested negative. He serves New Haven – does he ever!

Joe and I have been going to "Church" in the living room for months now and it looks like it will be even longer before we set foot indoors. We miss the services and our friends in Church, but the risk is too great for both of us, although Joe would insist it is all for me! Sitting on the couch for Mass is very relaxing though. We have become hermits. We only go out for doctors' appointments. Oh, and Joe does play golf! I told myself when this started that I'd have the cleanest closets in Bridgewater, but the truth is the desire for neatness wore off quickly. My reading took its place. Less stress on my now arthritic knees and back, left over from my fall two years ago. I thank that crazy dog, Maynard, daily for all he's done for me – or to me. Yet, he lives.

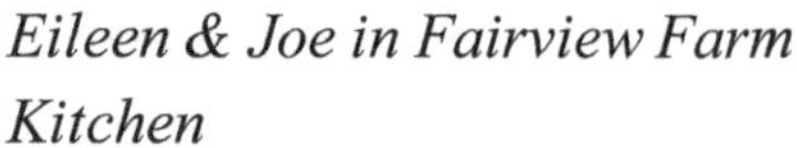

Eileen & Joe in Fairview Farm Kitchen

Front: David, Olivia, Jackson, Raven, Second: Mary Craddock, Brenda, Evelyn, Justin, Back: Ashley, Vance, Skylar, Melody, Derek

Christmas Countdown, 2021

From Eileen: We were optimistic for the end of Covid. For years, I have admired a 1946 Studebaker truck in neighboring Roxbury. It came down my driveway in January– a gift from Joe for our 52nd anniversary! Did I mention – it's ORANGE! I have named her "Wanda" and she is the proud recipient of TWO trophies so far! In our Bridgewater parade!

We welcomed a new puppy into the family for Easter. "Charlie" is a Chesapeake Bay retriever who wakes every morning exploding with enthusiasm and ready to greet the new day. We wish we had his energy!

Things looked good until June when Delta began. Soon, we were masked again. Despite my careful shenanigans, I managed to get a nasty case of pneumonia. Joe was, once again, my one-man band-chief cook and bottle washer. Once I got back on my feet, it was his turn – extensive dental surgery. We followed that up with a bunch of ugly health problems. By mutual agreement, we can now only have one member of the team sick at a time. Let's see how that works.

All these medical issues changed our summer plans, which included a trip to Denver to visit our granddaughters (and their parents!). A re-schedule was complicated by the vaccine not being available to children under 12. The girls are getting so big so fast! JoJo is in a special kindergarten program for gifted kids. It's the same one that Millie went through, so we know good things are waiting. The Buchheit Clan is ever busy with fun things to do – from road trips to concerts, they're always on the go!

The Carney Clan is doing well. Tim was promoted to Lieutenant and continues to fight fires in New Haven. Brigid is part way through her PhD in counseling with a specialty in PTSD among fire fighters. She is also teaching – a full plate. Flynn had her first paid gig, playing and singing on the green in Woodbridge. It went so well; she's been asked to join the players for "Fairfield Days". It will be delightful to see where her talents take her.

From Brenda:

The women filed into the large open room. Some were silent. Others made small talk as they walked. Everyone adjusted their mask. They knew what was in store for them. Newcomers seemed a little unsure. Each woman selected a mat from the side wall. Then, each woman took a seat on the floor.

Each woman had a hope. Transformation was the key. Each woman could picture herself looking like the instructor. It was a lot better than looking in the mirror. Brenda was one of these women. Although she had attended exercise classes for years, this was her first Pilates class. From what she understood, the focus of Pilates was that each movement comes from the core or abdominal region, building strength and endurance in the body.

That sounded good. The instructor described it as building a power belt rather than stomach bulk. As the hour progressed, Brenda noticed that her "power belt" was not like the instructor. Instead of a Gucci "belt," Brenda's was poochy.

All of us make attempts to change. Sometimes it is a New Year's resolution or sometimes it is a monthly new diet. We want clarity over the confusion, especially as we emerge into the "New Normal" resulting from the Covid pandemic. Just when we started to emerge from our homes, the Delta variant struck. Brenda decided to make health efforts a priority with a healthier diet and a hip replacement which went well.

One of the 2021 joys has been watching Justin and Raven's baby Olivia reach her first birthday and take walking steps. Her confidence has been bolstered by holding Daddy Justin's hand. Jackson continues to amaze with his dexterity both physically and mentally. His 3rd birthday party was a Bounce House which he never left for the several hours until its return.

Vance and Ashley saw their youngest start Kindergarten. David came home the first day and said, "Yes, he thought he'd go back." Evelyn was delighted also by her first day in Middle School (which is 5th grade) which offers new friends in every class--she's very social. Mary Craddock is happy with her 7th grade friends and looking forward to a New York/Paris trip with Gram Brenda, Evelyn, and her mom.

And Derek's Skylar has now graduated from The University of Texas, San Antonio. She emerged into the world of job hunting, rich with opportunity, but ragged with rejection. Success! She landed her first job in Colorado Springs starting at Christmas! Just as his nest was emptying, Derek had a major stroke in August. He is determined to recover to normal, and is aided energetically by Melody, but it is a long journey with small daily wins in physical therapy. He and Melody decided to move to Dallas where Brenda is welcoming them in her home to simplify the recovery. It has been a learning experience to be appreciative of small things, from the ability to swallow ice chips to walking upstairs easily.

Once again, we learn that our good health is such a blessing.

And so we come to a close . . .

There you have it. We have led you through a "countdown" calendar of 35 years to help you in the preparation for Christmas. The coming and going of the seasons reflects the coming and going of the circumstances of our lives. Our world is filled with calendars—ones for school and work, home, and family, for sports and social activities. Eileen and I suggest that our goal needs to be to keep Christmas in all four seasons, not just December 25. There is joy and a longing for life to be different, a time of hopeful anticipation throughout the year.

So, how do you keep the spirit of Christmas in all these seasons?

For Eileen's husband Joe, it is volunteerism for senior citizens. He has organized a volunteer team that helps the Senior Citizens in the community stay safe in their own home. For Eileen it is the Women's Guild of her church who prepare all year long for the Fall Craft Fair. For Eileen's granddaughter Flynn, now 14, it is spending time with family, taking a break from hectic "scheduled" events (Yes, this really is a quote when asked on a recent phone call).

Keeping the spirit of Christmas is being open to the insignificant things that we take for granted. Recently in Connecticut the unusual heat wave was so oppressive, there were health warnings. Eileen had dashed to the grocery in a fit of cabin fever, and then was returning to her car. She spotted her usual grocery cashier leaving for the day at the same time. Anna, the cashier, had only gone a few feet in the parking lot and was sweating profusely. Eileen stopped her car and asked her if she needed a ride home. Anna gratefully accepted. Eileen had no idea how far away she lived, and Anna just indicated to drive straight. As it turns out, it was the direction Eileen was driving. For Eileen, it was not out of her way. For Anna, it would have been a dangerous walk in the oppressive heat. The woman was grateful for the air-conditioned car that saved her from sweltering sun. Eileen was humbled because such a small action that really did not impact her made such a difference to Anna. These opportunities abound.

Brenda spent one Sunday talking to a homeless man at a church-sponsored lunch. She had helped equip new homes for several homeless who had recently moved to this city-sponsored housing. She listened to stories of having to acclimate by sleeping on a porch before moving inside to a mattress and bed in the city-sponsored housing. This man felt it was necessary to slowly acclimate to being inside a home due to years of being on the street. When she asked one man what his greatest adjustment was now that he had a house, he said it was getting over the fear of being stabbed or robbed while trying to sleep or that police would arrest him for vagrancy. But also, he admitted going back to his old haunts was not as satisfying because his good fortune of now having city-sponsored housing drove a wedge between him and his old homeless buddies. Brenda asked if he offered his porch to his old friends. He answered yes, but he knew it would only be accepted when the weather fell below freezing. They simply could not adjust to life off the streets. Unfortunately, another of the homeless she talked to mentioned that he was embarrassed to be sitting at lunch between two women when he knew he hadn't showered. That loss of dignity had not occurred to Brenda. She was thinking about the fact that he said this was the first meal he had in two days.

Truly listening and learning with the heart is part of Christmas and a way to make it last all year long. It is not a new thought. In "A Christmas Carol," Charles Dickens writes, "I will honour Christmas in my heart, and try to keep it all the year." Or from Roman's 15:13 "May the God of hope fill you with all joy and peace as you trust in him, so that you may overflow with hope by the power of the Holy Spirit."

Eileen and Brenda do not want to say good-bye. We are thinking about our next book. However, our Countdown is complete. We may have worries. The birds of care and problems fly above our heads. But we do not have to let them nest in our hair!

When you joined us in this journey, our children were young, and we had no idea of what the future held for us. We could not have imagined the births, deaths, successes, and failures, that life brings. It is the same with each of you.

We hope you recognized yourself and enjoyed coming along on insights from our journey. Our prayer is that you recognized the greater story of which we have all become a part. After all, the Bible is a love story. *Matthew tells us that having been warned in a dream not to return to Herod, the Magi departed for their country by another way (Matthew 2:11-12).* Their journey did not end there. Finding Jesus was their purpose, but they still had miles to go and wilderness experiences ahead of them in their journey. It is the same for us. Finding Jesus sets us on our way, but we have a lifetime of discovery, wonder, storms, and fog.

May the storms be around you but not within you. Oh, and Eileen and Brenda recommend your journey not be taken on a camel or dysfunctional donkey. Instead, we pray for a journey, alert and mindful, not of earning a "gold star" but focused on the guiding Star, leading to wonder, and Christmas joy all year round!

www.ingramcontent.com/pod-product-compliance
Lightning Source LLC
LaVergne TN
LVHW012052160826
845678LV00014B/2798

9798756334036